THE
EMERGENCY
SASQUATCH
ORDINANCE

THE
EMERGENCY SASQUATCH ORDINANCE

And Other Real Laws that Human Beings Have Actually
Dreamed Up, Enacted, and Sometimes Even Enforced

KEVIN UNDERHILL
Author of the Legal-Humor Blog *Lowering the Bar*

Printed in the United States of America.

17 16 15 14   5 4 3

Library of Congress Cataloging-in-Publication Data

Underhill, Kevin, author.
  The emergency Sasquatch ordinance and other real laws that human beings have actually dreamed up, enacted, and sometimes even enforced / Kevin Underhill.
    pages cm
  Includes bibliographical references.
  ISBN 978-1-62722-269-3 (alk. paper)
  1. Law—Humor. I. Title.
  K183.U53 2013
  340.02'07—dc23
                          2013046157

Discounts are available for books ordered in bulk. Special consideration is given to state bars, CLE programs, and other bar-related organizations. Inquire at Book Publishing, ABA Publishing, American Bar Association, 321 N. Clark Street, Chicago, Illinois 60654-7598.

www.ShopABA.org

Table of Contents

Introduction and Disclaimer

Throughout recorded history, human beings have created written laws in order to define the rights and obligations of those living within a particular society with regard to each other and to members of other societies, as well as to lesser creatures and other facets of the physical world. Any given set of laws reflects not only the unique rules and customs of the particular society in which it was created, but also certain relationships and ideas that are common in one way or another to all human beings.

And just like human beings, they are sometimes weird and stupid.

In this book, you will find a collection of written laws. Strange as it will seem at times, each one was actually thought up by one or more real human beings who then, in most cases, decided after writing it down and upon further reflection that, yes, this *would* be a good rule that everybody should follow from now on. Many of these rules turned out to be dumb.

It is possible that in some cases, a law only *seems* dumb because we are so far removed from that society's cultural context, but often I think we can have some confidence that it was pretty dumb to begin with. In some cases, the law itself may make some sense but only because human beings are dumb, or at least strange. In a few cases, the law is in this book just because I thought it was funny. That's the kind of thing you get to do when you write a book: decide what goes in it. And in two cases, the person responsible for the law was actually *trying* to be funny when he wrote it. Or maybe all these people were trying, but only two succeeded. Hard to say.

Laws don't have to be in writing, of course, which is good because for a long time nobody knew how to write. There were (and still are) unwritten laws, of course. For example, the first law ever was probably some unwritten version of "thou shalt not kill." (The second was "except for Neanderthals.") But obviously we don't have evidence today of laws they didn't write down. The ancient Egyptians could write, but they wrote mostly on papyrus, which doesn't last very long and so none of their law codes have survived. Therefore, although the Egyptians probably had some pretty weird laws—remember, these were people who would pull your brain out through your nose, wrap you in bandages, and bury you under a mountain, and that was if they *liked* you—they will appear only in this introduction.

The book therefore begins with the laws of ancient Sumeria and Babylon. The Sumerians and Babylonians were basically contemporaries of the Egyptians, but unlike the Egyptians, they generally wrote on tablets of baked clay or on various stone things. Their law clerks probably died young, but on the plus side, what they wrote was more or less fossilized for us to make fun of thousands of years later. So it all evens out.

We then move on to the laws of the Hittites, who were quite strange, and those of the ancient Greeks and Romans, as well as a few examples from medieval times.

Note that all the ancient laws discussed here are of course translations from languages other than English. Translations can vary a lot, and when there was a choice I picked the translation I thought was funnier. That's because this book is for entertainment purposes. If you are looking for something with greater intellectual heft, you might want to put this book down, adjust your monocle, and head over to a more highbrow section of the bookstore, Professor Brainiac. How about something on particle physics or maybe existential Serbian drama? Ooh, I know, how about "Film Studies"? Hey, look at me, everyone, I'm browsing through scholarly works on French cinema of the 1940s! It's for my paper relating it to Eisenstein and the avant-garde movement during the Weimar Republic! Ooooh!

Sorry. I didn't get into film school.

Most of the book is composed of laws that have been inflicted on the population of the United States. This is solely because that is the country in which I live and in which I am, probably due to some clerical error, actually licensed to practice law. Note that not all 50 states are represented in this book, but *that* is only because of time constraints, not because any states have laws that all make perfect sense. So quit looking all smug, Vermont.

The book then concludes with a selection of modern(ish) laws from other countries, some of which have a legal system similar to that of the United States (the United Kingdom, Australia, New Zealand, and so on), some of which have a completely different tradition (Germany, China, Papua New Guinea), and some of which can barely be said to observe the "rule of law" at all (Canada). Some of those laws are also available to me only in translation, and for that reason and others, you are cautioned that as to the international section in particular I could fairly be accused of winging it.

Which leads to an important point, perhaps the most important one in this entire book: *Nothing in this book should be acted upon or considered legal advice.* I'm not too worried about you following my interpretation of the Code of Hammurabi (although please don't), but this book does discuss many laws that are currently in force (at the time of writing) and I often interpret them or give my opinions about them. You should remember that although I usually do know what I'm talking about, I'm also a lawyer and so I am trained to *sound* like I know what I'm talking about even when I don't. So, for example, if you decide to take home a 20-foot whale you found in Scotland without offering it to the Queen first, or to follow my suggestions about how to avoid joining a posse in South Carolina, you do so at your own risk.

Finally, although this will seem impossible, all of the laws mentioned in this book are (or were) real. (In a few cases the law was proposed but not enacted, but if I didn't make exceptions for those, then I could not have included, for example, the New Mexico Expert Wizard Bill of 1995, and that would have been a tragedy.) That distinguishes this book from most of the other "dumb laws" books and websites you might come across, which often repeat what are basically urban legends. My personal feeling is that if it isn't true, it cannot be truly dumb.

With that explanation (and *legally binding disclaimer*), please enjoy this book. That's assuming this copy already belongs to you. If it doesn't, at this point you really should buy it or put it back where you found it. Or, if you have been reading this over someone's shoulder, now would be a good time to start pretending to do something else before this person turns around.

Too late.

—Kevin Underhill

PART ONE

In Ancient Times

The first written law code we know about mentions beer.

We don't actually have a copy of the laws enacted by Urukagina, who ruled the Sumerian city-state of Lagash over 4,000 years ago. But we know they existed because later sources refer to them, and Urukagina himself referred to them in what is called the "Reform Edict," in which he reminded everybody how bad things had been before he came along, and how much better they got once he took charge.

If you are thinking that politicians always say that kind of thing, you are correct. This is our first piece of evidence that people haven't really changed all that much over the centuries, and so accordingly we will see a number of common themes and topics recurring in this survey.

Example: For more than 40 centuries now, human beings have enjoyed getting drunk. That makes beer valuable and (if you haven't invented money yet) useful for bartering. Urukagina wanted to make sure people remembered how much more expensive things were before his reforms. Back in the day, the Reform Edict says, it was super-expensive just to have someone buried:

> For a corpse being brought to the grave,
> his beer was seven jugs, and his bread 420 loaves.
> Two barig of hazi-barley, one woolen garment,
> one lead goat, and one bed the undertaker took away,
> and one barig of barley the person(s) of . . . took away.

That is, to have someone buried, you had to pay the undertakers and priests *seven* jugs of beer. (Also, 420 loaves of bread and some barley and a shirt and a bed and a goat, but whatever.)

Once Urukagina showed up, though, things were different:

> For a corpse being brought to the grave,
> his beer will be 3 jugs and his bread eighty loaves.
> One bed and one lead goat the undertaker shall take away,
> and three ban of barley the person(s) of . . . shall take away.

That's almost a 60 percent cut in estate beer taxes.

Reform Edict of Urukagina (ca. 2350 B.C.).

Here we see part of the first known law code . . .
No, wait, this was just someone doodling.

Hammurabi was not a guy to mess around with.

The Code of Hammurabi is the oldest law code preserved in any detail. In fact, we have a nearly complete copy, thanks to Hammurabi being thoughtful enough to have it carved in stone and buried for us to read later. Hammurabi was the sixth ruler of the First Dynasty of Babylon, and, at least according to him, he was divinely chosen to bring justice:

> [T]he gods Anu and Enlil, for the enhancement of the well-being of the people, named me by my name: Hammurabi, the pious prince, who venerates the gods, to make justice prevail in the land, to abolish the wicked and the evil, to prevent the strong from oppressing the weak, to rise like the sun-god Shumash over all humankind, to illuminate the land.

It goes on for several feet like that, so humility is apparently the one virtue he didn't have. He was serious about bringing justice, though, or at least about writing down the rules that defined justice in the land illuminated by his godlike radiance.

His code is known for its eye-for-an-eye penalty, but that was Hammurabi being *lenient*. Fines were imposed for many offenses, but the death penalty was anything but rare:

> If any one ensnare another, putting a ban upon him [i.e., make false charges against him], but he cannot prove it, then he that ensnared him shall be put to death.

If any one take a male or female slave of the court, or . . . of a freed man, outside the city gates, he shall be put to death.

If any one buy from the son or slave of another man, without witnesses or a contract, . . . he is considered a thief and shall be put to death.

If any one break a hole into a house [i.e., commit a burglary], he shall be put to death before that hole and be buried.

If fire break out in a house, and some one who comes to put it out [steals property], he shall be thrown into that . . . fire.

You get the idea.

Code of Hammurabi, §§ 1, 7, 15, 21, 25 (ca. 1780 B.C.).[1]

"And the penalty for insulting the royal hat shall be—"
"Death, O King?"
"Let me finish."

Babylonian judges were fired after their first mistake.

Possibly because its penalties could be so harsh (that's the first of the many speculations I'll be offering in this book), the Code of Hammurabi provided that a judge who made a mistake—apparently just one—was fined and permanently removed from the bench:

> If a judge try a case, reach a decision, and present his judgment in writing; if later error shall appear in his decision, and it be through his own fault, then he shall pay twelve times the fine set by him in the case, and he shall be publicly removed from the judge's bench, and never again shall he sit there to render judgment.

Assuming they applied that law strictly, it could have been a powerful incentive for judges to render careful and just decisions. On the other hand, since they had to write everything out on baked-clay or stone tablets, maybe they just didn't want to have to make any corrections. Ever.

Code of Hammurabi, § 5.

But the river was never wrong.

Babylonian life was dominated by the Euphrates River, and so maybe it is not surprising that it played a role in the legal system as well. A number of provisions in the Code refer to what has been called the river ordeal, which was sometimes optional, sometimes mandatory. This one, for example, was apparently the procedure followed if one person accused another of sorcery:

> If any one bring an accusation against a man, and the accused go to the river and leap into the river, if he sink in the river his accuser shall take possession of his house. But if the river prove that the accused is not guilty, and he escape unhurt, then he who had brought the accusation shall be put to death, while he who leaped into the river shall take possession of the house that had belonged to his accuser.

Got that? If someone accuses you of sorcery, you go jump in the river. If you sink . . . well, you sink, and the accuser gets all your stuff (except what you had on you when you jumped, I assume). But if the river comes through for you, the accuser dies, and you get all *his* stuff.

My guess is that there were few if any lawyers in ancient Babylon, because it would have made a lot more sense to spend that money on swimming lessons.

Code of Hammurabi, § 2.

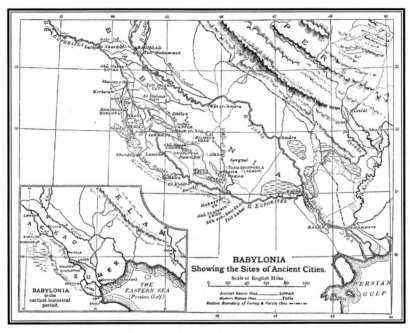

Mesopotamia: It was hot and violent 4,000 years ago, too.

The river frequently
judged women.

Men sometimes got the river ordeal, or could choose it as an option, but it sounds like Babylonian women spent an awful lot of time in the Euphrates. For example:

> If a [female] tavern-keeper does not accept corn according to gross weight in payment of drink, but takes money, and the price of the drink is less than that of the corn, she shall be convicted and thrown into the water.
>
> ***
>
> If the "finger is pointed" at a man's wife about another man, but she is not caught sleeping with the other man, she shall jump into the river for her husband.
>
> ***
>
> If a man is taken prisoner in war, and there is a sustenance in his house, but his wife leave house and court, and go to another house: because this wife did not keep her court, and went to another house, she shall be judicially condemned and thrown into the water.

Note the relative leniency of that second one. Apparently, if there was no actual *proof* of the rumor that the woman had cheated on her husband (the "finger is pointed" but she wasn't caught in the act), they would let her jump into the river herself instead of throwing her. So it's not like they were being totally unreasonable about this.

Code of Hammurabi, §§ 108, 132–33.

Babylonian doctors also ran some serious risks.

Here's one along the lines of the famous eye-for-an-eye rule . . . sort of:

> If a physician make a large incision with an operating knife and cure it, or if he open a tumor (over the eye) with an operating knife, and saves the eye, he shall receive ten shekels in money.
>
> ***
>
> If a physician make a large incision with the operating knife, and kill him, or open a tumor with the operating knife, and cut out the eye, his hands shall be cut off.

Given the obvious risks of a malpractice claim, you have to wonder just how many eye doctors they had in Babylon. "You know, it looks bad but I think it might get better on its own. Actually, why don't you see if Dr. Sargon is available?"

On the one hand, 10 shekels was apparently a pretty good payday; according to another section of the Code, a boat cost just two shekels. On the other hand (assuming you still have both hands), building five boats seems like a much safer way to earn some shekels.

Code of Hammurabi, §§ 215, 218.

The Hittites apparently stole each other's doors.

After the Babylonians came the Hittites, who seem to have been significantly weirder.

For example, the existence of the following law suggests that it was not uncommon for a Hittite who got mad at somebody to go over and steal that person's front door:

> If anyone steals a door as a result of a quarrel, he shall replace everything that may get lost in the house, and he shall pay one mina [40 shekels] of silver.

If something "got lost" because the door was gone, then presumably somebody took it. But notice that the door-stealer in this scenario isn't being charged with taking anything but the door itself. Someone else must have taken the other stuff. And it also seems fair to assume that this happened repeatedly, to the point where someone felt the need for a law to try to deter it. So what this law tells us, or at least what I am going to conclude from it, is that rather than settle their disputes in some grown-up way the Hittites would run around stealing each other's doors in hopes that some passing burglar would do the rest.

This is an odd way to run a vendetta, to say the least. If you're already willing to steal, and you want your enemy to lose his stuff, why not just take the stuff? Then you don't have to rely on some third-party burglar. Plus, if you're running down the street carrying a door, people can probably guess what you're up to, and if you do make it home then there's the problem of explaining the extra door you've got sitting around. How about this: just leave the door *open* and be on your way. You don't actually need to take it with you.

Doors had been around for thousands of years at this point, so that's no excuse. You'd think they'd have worked all this out by the Bronze Age.

The Laws of the Hittites, § 170 (c. 1650–1500 B.C.).[2]

For Hittite men, some partners were strictly off-limits, others . . . not.

The door-stealing thing was odd, but compared to some other Hittite customs it seems totally sensible. For example, consider the Hittite approach to certain sexual transgressions:

> If a man have intercourse with a cow, it is a capital crime, he shall die. . . . If a man have intercourse with a sheep, it is a capital crime, he shall die. . . . If anyone have intercourse with a pig or a dog, he shall die.

Okay, don't touch the animals, got it. Death penalty, got it. But:

> If a man have intercourse with a horse or a mule, there is no punishment. But he shall not approach the king, and shall not become a priest.

As far as I can tell, no one has any idea why the Hittites distinguished between cows, sheep, pigs, and dogs on the one hand, and horses and mules on the other. Consorting with a member of the first group was a capital crime, but consorting with a horse or mule incurred no penalty at all. True, the offender could never become a priest and the king wouldn't want to be seen in any carvings with him, but most people would not have been hobnobbing in those circles to begin with.

This is like saying that if you get caught robbing a bank, you can never be the Pope. It just doesn't seem like much of a deterrent.

Then there was this law, which seems to demonstrate at least a slightly more elevated status for foreign women—men could apparently hit on them freely:

> If any man have intercourse with a foreign woman and pick up
> this one, now that one, there is no punishment.

The explanation may be that cows, sheep, pigs, and dogs were considered particularly unclean for reasons we don't understand; horses, mules, and foreigners, not so much. But no one really knows.

The Laws of the Hittites, §§ 187–88, 199, 200a.[3]

I am not to blame, Your Honor, for the pig sprang upon *me*.

Did I say that last group of laws was strange? This is where it gets truly weird, because in certain cases, it was considered the animal's fault:

> If an ox spring upon a man for intercourse, the ox shall die but the man shall not die. One sheep shall be fetched as a substitute for the man, and they shall kill it. If a pig spring upon a man for intercourse, there is no punishment.

Now, I've seen a dog hump someone's leg. That can be a little uncomfortable, but no big deal. Not that I spend much time around oxen and pigs—especially now—but I have yet to see one "spring upon a man for intercourse."

Does that happen?

Were oxen and pigs in the habit of "springing upon" Hittite men who were just minding their own business, or was something else going on here?

Why were oxen punished but not pigs?

And what the hell did the sheep do wrong?

We may never know. Or want to know.

The Laws of the Hittites, § 199.

In early Rome, having a conflict of interest could be a capital offense.

Lawyers, politicians, and a number of similar life-forms are not allowed to take positions or get in situations that could put their interests in conflict with those of a client. If that happens, it is (creatively) known as a conflict of interest.

The Romans had rules like this dating back to the very founding of the city — or at least that's what they claimed later on, since nothing was actually written down until long afterward. But if the story is true, then Romulus (the first king, according to legend) took conflicts of interest pretty damn seriously:

1. After Romulus had distinguished the persons of higher rank from those of inferior condition, then he passed laws and apportioned the duties for each to do. . . . He entrusted and gave the plebeians to the patricians by permitting each plebeian . . . to choose for his patron the patrician whom he wished . . . and by calling this protection patronage.

2. [T]he patricians were required to interpret the law for their own clients; . . . to bring suit on behalf of clients when wronged; . . . and to support them in the action. . . . In common to both it was neither holy nor lawful to bring suit, to testify, or to cast a vote [as a juror?] the one against the other. . . . He who was convicted of doing any of these things was held by the law of treason, which Romulus enacted, so that

it was lawful for anyone to slay the person convicted of this crime, as a sacrifice to the god of the underworld.

There was more to the Roman patron-client relationship than legal representation, but that was a big part of it. The extra "patronage" element is missing today, but we also don't hand out the death penalty for conflicts of interest. Normally, a conflicted lawyer or law firm is just disqualified from working on the case in question, and that is enough these days to satisfy the god of the underworld. Who, to be honest, has really gotten kind of lazy.

Laws of the Kings, I Romulus, §§ 1–2 (ca. 725 B.C.).[4]

In Athens, each side got 10 gallons on the water-clock to make its case.

The ancient Athenians had jury trials, and an elaborate system of choosing jurors to make sure service was random. They also understood the wisdom, as we do today (most of the time), of giving the parties only a limited amount of time to make their cases:

> These preliminaries being concluded, the cases are called on. If it is a day for private cases, the private litigants are called. Four cases are taken in each of the categories defined in the law, and the litigants swear to confine their speeches to the point at issue.

Yeah, litigants do that today, too. Good luck with that one.

> If it is a day for public causes, the public litigants are called, and only one case is tried. Water-clocks are provided, having small supply-tubes, into which the water is poured by which the length of the pleadings is regulated. Ten gallons are allowed for a case in which an amount of more than five thousand drachmas is involved, and three for the second speech on each side. When the amount is between one and five thousand drachmas, seven gallons are allowed for the first speech and two for the second; when it is less than one thousand, five and two. Six gallons are allowed for arbitrations between rival claimants, in which there is no second speech. The official chosen by lot to superintend

the water-clock places his hand on the supply tube whenever the clerk is about to read a resolution or law or affidavit or treaty. When, however, a case is conducted according to a set measurement of the day, he does not stop the supply, but each party receives an equal allowance of water. . . . The measured day is employed in cases when imprisonment, death, exile, loss of civil rights, or confiscation of goods is assigned as the penalty.

We use digital instead of water-clocks today, of course, but we have exactly the same difficulty getting people to shut up.

Aristotle, The Athenian Constitution, pt. 67 (ca. 350 B.C.).

Athenian juries had up to 1,500 members.

American courts often have trouble finding 12 people for jury duty, but in ancient Athens, juries typically had at least 500 members and sometimes a lot more:

> Most of the courts consist of 500 members . . . ; and when it is necessary to bring public cases before a jury of 1,000 members, two courts combine for the purpose, the most important cases of all are brought 1,500 jurors, or three courts.

They voted by tossing bronze disks into urns, in such a way that each juror's vote remained secret:

> When the speeches are concluded, the officials assigned to the taking of the votes give each juror two [ballots], one pierced and one solid. . . .
>
> When the jurors are about to vote, the crier demands first whether the litigants enter a protest against any of the evidence; for no protest can be received after the voting has begun. Then he proclaims again, "The pierced ballot for the plaintiff, the solid for the defendant"; and the juror, taking his two [ballots] from the stand, with his hand closed over the stem so as not to show either the pierced or the solid ballot to the litigants, casts the one which is to count into the brazen urn, and the other into the wooden urn.

Whichever [party] has the majority is victorious; but if the votes are equal the verdict is for the defendant.

So far it's 6–1 for the defendant.

There were only about 30,000 to 40,000 citizens in Athens, and 6,000 were selected for the jury pool every year. So it was a great place to live if you enjoyed jury duty. On the other hand, what else were you going to spend your time doing? Arguing with Socrates? Fighting the Spartans? Neither of those were a whole lot of fun, either.

Aristotle, The Athenian Constitution, pts. 68 & 69.[5]

The original meaning of "strip search."

Both the Greeks and Romans allowed someone who claimed that another person had stolen his property to go into the suspect's house to search for it. But, apparently to make sure the searcher didn't plant something and then claim that it had been stolen, he had to strip before going inside:

15a. The penalty for detected and planted theft shall be triple damages. . . .

15b. . . . by platter and by loincloth.

I know it doesn't quite say that, but bear with me.

According to the editors of *Ancient Roman Statutes*, these two laws "were apparently obscure, even to [later] Roman commentators." That is, some Romans writing centuries later (and presumably having the full text, which we don't) interpreted the Latin in 15b (nudus, licio cinctus, lancem habens) as meaning "nude, except for a loincloth," though it may have meant only "lightly clad [i.e., no toga] and carrying a platter."

It is likely that they were talking about getting nudus in order to search someone's house because we know the Greeks had a similar rule or custom: In Aristophanes' comedy *The Clouds*, Socrates tells someone to take off his cloak before going inside and the man responds, "But I'm not here to look for stolen goods."

It was probably a lot funnier in 419 B.C.

Still, the joke serves as evidence that the custom existed. People planning to search for allegedly stolen items were asked to strip, presumably to make sure they weren't going to try to smuggle something inside. At least, nobody can think of another reason for this requirement.

Nobody seems to have a clue what the platter, if there really was one, might have been for. Did the searcher have to carry the item out on a platter if he found it? What if it was too big for that? And what if the thing that got stolen was a platter?

Just some of the unanswered questions that remain, if you still need an idea for your thesis.

Table VIII, Torts or Delicts (ratified 449 B.C.).[6]

There was no crying at Roman funerals.

The Twelve Tables were early Roman laws that dealt with subjects like civil procedure, property, and family law. (As the previous item showed, they also covered certain torts.) The tenth table, in which the following laws were contained, gives us a pretty good idea that the Romans were not big on people getting all worked up about funerals:

3. Expenses of a funeral shall be limited to three mourners wearing veils and one mourner wearing an inexpensive purple tunic and ten flutists. . . .
4. Women shall not tear their cheeks or shall not make a sorrowful outcry on account of a funeral.
5a. A dead person's bones shall not be collected that one may make a second funeral.
5b. An exception is for death in battle and on foreign soil.
6a. Anointing by slaves is abolished and every kind of drinking bout . . . there shall be no costly sprinkling, no long garlands, no incense boxes . . .
6b. A myrrh-spiced drink . . . shall not be poured on a dead person.
7. Whoever wins a crown himself or by his property, by honor, or by valor, the crown is bestowed on him at his burial . . .

8. No gold shall be added to a corpse. But if any one buries or burns a corpse that has gold dental work it shall be without prejudice.

Number 6b suggests it was acceptable to pour a drink on the departed; they just didn't want you showing off by wasting the good stuff.

Later on, Cicero complained that people of his time were starting to get carried away again:

> [W]e learned the Twelve Tables when schoolboys, as an indispensable lesson, which, by–the–bye, no one attends to now–a–days. Let extravagance, therefore, be diminished to three suits of mourning, with purple bands, and ten flute players. Excessive lamentations are also to be prohibited by this rule. . . . These rules are very commendable, and equally practicable by the rich and poor, and they are eminently conformable to nature, who sweeps away by mortality all the distinctions of fortune.

It does seem like 10 flute players is more than enough, to be honest.

Table X, Sacred Law, §§ 1–8.[7]

Romans also had to keep an eye on wandering trees.

The Roman emperor Justinian was famous for a number of things, such as reconquering parts of the Western Empire, fighting the Persians, and sending in the legions to stomp a bunch of rude sports fans who unwisely insulted him one day at the chariot races. One of his less violent deeds was to supervise a reorganization of Roman law that became known as the Corpus Juris Civilis, often called the Code of Justinian. They would probably call it that when he was around, anyway, especially after the whole chariot thing.

It covered all the things you would expect such a code to cover, but its property section had this unusual rule about wandering trees:

> But if the violence of a river should bear away a portion of your land and unite it to the land of your neighbor, it undoubtedly still continues [to be] yours. If, however, it remains for long united to your neighbor's land, and the trees, which it swept away with it, take root in his ground, these trees from that time become part of your neighbor's estate.

I guess that rule is fine; it just makes you wonder how often this migrating-tree problem actually occurred, if they felt they had to include a specific rule about it in the Code. The lesson, of course, is that if there's a flood, you need to go out and round up your trees before they take root someplace else. If you wait that long, you're out of luck.

Code of Justinian, Book II, pt. I, § 21 (534 C.E.).

PART TWO

In Post-Ancient but Pre-Modern Times

Under the Salic law, the fine for hitting somebody depended on how hard you hit him.

The law of the Salian Franks (also just called the Salic law) imposed fines for almost every sort of offense, including murder. This general idea was not at all uncommon, but some of the Salic specifics are weird.

For example, the fines for battery depended on how hard you hit the person, but they don't seem entirely consistent:

CONCERNING WOUNDS

4. He who hits another man on the head so that his blood falls to the ground, and it is proved against him, shall be liable to pay six hundred denarii.

5. He who strikes another man on the head so that the brain shows, and it is proved against him, shall be liable to pay six hundred denarii.

6. If the three bones that lie over the brain protrude, he shall be liable to pay twelve hundred denarii.

❋ ❋ ❋

8. If a freeman strikes another freeman with a stick but the blood does not flow, for up to three blows, he shall be liable to pay three hundred sixty denarii, that is, for each blow he shall always pay one hundred twenty denarii.

If those numbers are correct, somebody planning to hit hard enough to draw blood might as well go ahead and hit a little harder—it doesn't cost any extra. Unless he really overdoes it so that the bones poke out, because that's twice as much. Personally I'd combine numbers five and six and just make any brain-infringing blow a 1,200-denarii offense.

I like number eight because it allows you the flexibility to decide how many blows with a stick you can afford.

Pactus Legis Salicae XVII (ca. 500).[8]

Concerning the man who touches the hand or arm or finger of a free woman.

Here's some more evidence that the Franks needed to work on the schedule of fines a little more:

1. The freeman who touches the hand or arm or finger of a free woman or of any other woman, and it is proved against him, shall be liable to pay six hundred denarii.
2. If he touches her arm below the elbow, he shall be liable to pay twelve hundred denarii.
3. But if he places his hand above her elbow and it is proved against him, he shall be liable to pay fourteen hundred denarii.

Just as a reminder, 1,200 denarii was also the fine for whacking somebody over the head hard enough to make his skull bones protrude. Touching the upper arm was more expensive than that?

God forbid you should try to get to second base.

Pactus Legis Salicae XX.

Concerning abusive terms.

People have always called each other names, but the names they call each other have—to some extent—changed over the years:

1. He who calls someone else a pederast shall be liable to pay six hundred denarii.
2. He who claims that someone else is covered in dung shall be liable to pay one hundred twenty denarii.
3. He who calls a free woman or man a prostitute and cannot prove it shall be liable to pay eighteen hundred denarii.
4. He who calls someone else a fox shall be liable to pay one hundred twenty denarii.
5. He who calls someone else a rabbit shall be liable to pay one hundred twenty denarii.
6. The freeman who accuse[s] another man of throwing down his shield and running away, and cannot prove it, shall be liable to pay one hundred twenty denarii.
7. He who calls someone else an informer or liar and cannot prove it shall be liable to pay six hundred denarii.

Being called a pederast was obviously a serious insult, though the Franks apparently considered calling someone a prostitute to be three times as bad. Seems like it should be the other way around, but they may have seen this differently in the sixth century. Calling someone a fox also didn't mean what it means today, or at least what it meant in the 1970s. The meaning of "rabbit" as a term of abuse is a little puzzling—we might think of that as something like "coward" ("running like a rabbit") but that's what the next item on the list was for. Rabbits also reproduce very quickly, but that doesn't seem like a 120-denarii insult.

Most likely your main question at this point is: What's the Latin for "person covered in dung"? I think the answer is *concagatum*, but you should consult an expert before deploying this one.

Pactus Legis Salicae XXX.

Concerning sorcerers and witches.

This would also seem to fit in the section on abusive terms, except for the very weird last item:

1. He who calls another man a sorcerer [herburgium]—that is, . . . one who is said to carry a brass cauldron in which witches brew—if he is not able to prove it, he shall be liable to pay twenty-five hundred denarii.
2. He who calls a free woman a witch and is not able to prove it shall be liable to pay three times twenty-five hundred denarii [or seventy-five hundred denarii, obviously].
3. If a witch eats a man and it is proved against her, she shall be liable to pay eight thousand denarii.

Okay, Franks, I was with you on the first couple, given that calling somebody a sorcerer or a witch in medieval times could have pretty serious consequences. Then you lost me on number three.

Many actual experts are confused about this one, too. Some sources translate it as "proved against *him*" and "*he* shall be liable to pay," which makes even less sense. If a witch eats a man, why is that his fault, and how would you collect from the guy anyway? But changing it to "against her" doesn't clarify much.

Maybe "eats a man" translates to something like "possesses" or "casts a spell over," although I would have assumed that if that could actually be proved, they'd be having themselves a bonfire, not collecting a fine.

Pactus Legis Salicae LXIV.

Concerning those who are poor but not so poor they don't own a fence.

As mentioned above, the Frankish system focused on setting fines, which was not unusual historically, even for serious crimes. Clearly, though, if somebody just couldn't pay the fine, the Franks were pretty much out of good ideas at that point:

> If any one have killed a man, and, having given up all his property, has not enough to comply with the full terms of the law, he shall present 12 sworn witnesses to the effect that, neither above the earth nor under it, has he any more property than he has already given. And he shall afterwards go into his house, and shall collect in his hand dust from the four corners of it, and shall afterwards stand upon the threshold, looking inwards into the house. And then, with his left hand, he shall throw over his shoulder some of that dust on the nearest relative that he has. But if his father and (his father's) brothers have already paid, he shall then throw that dust on their (the brothers') children—that is, over three (relatives) who are nearest on the father's and three on the mother's side. And after that, in his shirt, without girdle and without shoes, a staff in his hand, he shall spring over the hedge. And then those three shall pay half of what is lacking. . . .

I'm thinking that some wise-ass scribe put in the line about "springing over the hedge" as a practical joke, and then died before he could tell anybody he was just kidding.

Another source translates this phrase as "he should go jump over his fence," but that's just as ridiculous. Same for the thing with the dust. Just let the guy ask to borrow the money, okay? That can be embarrassing enough without all the jumping around.

Pactus Legis Salicae LVIII.

The value of a
Russian mustache.

Fines were also imposed for most offenses in medieval Russia, including some extremely violent ones, as the following list shows:

> If a person hits another with a stick, or a rod, or a fist, or a bowl, or a drinking horn, or the dull side of a sword, he is to pay twelve grivnas; if the offender is not hit back [by his victim], he must pay, and there the matter ends.
>
> If a person strikes another with an unsheathed sword, or with the hilt of a sword, he pays twelve grivnas for the offense.
>
> If a person hits [another's] arm and the arm is severed or shrinks, he pays forty grivnas. And if he hits the leg [but does not sever it], and then he [the victim] becomes lame, let both [parties] reach an agreement.
>
> And if a finger is cut off, three grivnas for the offense.
>
> For the mustache twelve grivnas; and for the beard twelve grivnas.

You'd think only a really spectacular mustache would be worth the same as four fingers, but the law doesn't say anything about mustache evaluation. Maybe that was up to a judge. (Note: It's hard to say exactly how much a grivna would be in today's currency. One source I found said that one grivna equalled 4 wiarduneks, 24 skojecs, 240 denarii, or 480 obols, if that helps at all.)

Traditionally, Russians did feel pretty strongly about facial hair, though. In 1705, Peter the Great decided to ban the beard entirely, because he was trying to Westernize the country and thought beards were antiquated. The reaction was so strong that he had to back down (and he's not called Peter the Timid). He imposed a beard tax instead, so men could keep the beard as long as they paid and carried around a beard token, like the one pictured, in order to prove it.

If that's what they looked like,
no wonder he wanted to ban them.

Russkaia Pravda (short version), arts. 4, 7 & 8 (ca. 1050 A.D.).[9]

The first to tar and feather?

It may have been Richard I of England, who issued this law before setting out (by sea) for the Third Crusade, hoping to keep the Crusaders under control on the way there:

> Richard by the grace of God king of England, and duke of Normandy and Aquitaine, and count of Anjou, to all his subjects who are about to go by sea to Jerusalem, greeting.
>
> Know that we, by the common counsel of upright men, have made the laws here given. Whoever slays a man on ship board shall be bound to the dead man and thrown into the sea. But if he shall slay him on land, he shall be bound to the dead man and buried in the earth. If any one, moreover, shall be convicted through lawful witnesses of having drawn a knife to strike another, or of having struck him so as to draw blood, he shall lose his hand. But if he shall strike him with his fist without drawing blood, he shall be dipped three times in the sea. But if any one shall taunt or insult a comrade or charge him with hatred of God: as many times as he shall have insulted him, so many ounces of silver shall he pay.
>
> A robber, moreover, convicted of theft, shall be shorn like a hired fighter, and boiling tar shall be poured over his head, and feathers from a cushion shall be shaken out over his head, so that he may be publicly known; and at the first land where the ships put in he shall be cast on shore.

According to one source, this is the first recorded appearance of tarring and feathering as a punishment. It was still popular a few centuries later in what was about to become the United States, but (somewhat surprisingly), it is not currently the law in any part of the country.

At least not officially.

Laws of Richard I (Coeur de Lion) Concerning Crusaders
Who Were to Go by Sea (1190 A.D.).[10]

Richard's strict anti-violence position evolved over time.

PART THREE

The Laws of the
United States

Congress recently banned "lunatics."

The first section of the United States Code, the multivolume compilation of federal statutes, defines terms that are used in other sections of the Code. For example, when the word "officer" is used, it means "any person authorized by law to perform the duties of the office." Doesn't really seem that helpful, but it's there if you need it.

Until recently, the section also said this:

> [T]he words "insane" and "insane person" and "lunatic" shall include every idiot, lunatic, insane person, and person non compos mentis [not of sound mind]. . . .

Then Congress passed and the president signed the "21st Century Language Act of 2012," the sole purpose of which was to remove the word "lunatic" from the Code, on the grounds that it is outdated and now generally is used only as an insult. As a result, the law now reads:

> [T]he words "insane" and "insane person" shall include every idiot, insane person, and person non compos mentis. . . .

So lunatics are out.

Only one member of Congress voted against the bill: Rep. Louie Gohmert (R-Texas). Gohmert, who ironically is kind of a nut, issued a statement explaining that he had voted "no" because, "not only should we not [bother to] eliminate the word 'lunatic' from federal law when the most pressing issue of the day is saving our country from bankruptcy, we should use the word to describe the people who want to continue with business as usual in Washington."

Luckily, the definition still includes "idiot."

1 U.S.C. § 1.[11]

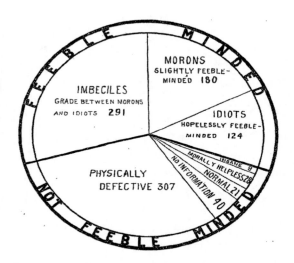

The surprising thing about this study is that they actually found 21 "normal" people in Congress.

Fear of "infamy" is not a good reason to avoid testifying before Congress.

Actually, it may be a great reason to avoid that if you can, but it's not a valid legal reason:

> No witness is privileged to refuse to testify to any fact, or to produce any paper, respecting which he shall be examined by either House of Congress, or by a joint committee established by a joint or concurrent resolution of the two Houses of Congress, or by any committee of either House, upon the ground that his testimony to such fact or his production of such paper may tend to disgrace him or otherwise render him infamous.

For a long time it wasn't clear whether Congress had the authority to punish anyone other than its own members. There's nothing about it in the Constitution. But in 1821 the Supreme Court held that Congress has the "implied" power to hold a nonmember in contempt (in that case, for attempted bribery) and imprison that person until that legislative session ends.

The extent to which this applied to witnesses at congressional hearings, or even whether Congress could require witnesses to testify at all, was still not clear. That didn't stop Congress from holding witnesses in contempt and locking them up, which it did a number of times, occasionally using rooms in the Capitol as cells.

Back in the day, Congress didn't hold hearings very often—although now it doesn't seem to do much else—so the issue rarely came up and questions about contempt and privilege were never definitively answered. In 1857, Congress finally passed a law saying that witnesses did indeed have to answer its questions and (similar to the above) could not assert a privilege based on fear of "infamy." (Note: passing a law is a pretty good way to settle a debate, if you have that option.)

Although the Supreme Court had to get involved again (not surprisingly, during the McCarthy years) to ensure it, those testifying before Congress do still have privileges based on the First and Fifth amendments, which is nice.

2 U.S.C. §§ 192–93.[12]

Dairy farmers get reimbursed for fallout contamination, as long as it's not their fault.

A federal law passed in 1968 authorizes payments to dairy farmers who are forced to take milk off the market due to certain kinds of contamination. They don't get paid, though, if the contamination is their fault:

> The Secretary of Agriculture is authorized to make indemnity payments for milk or cows producing such milk at a fair market value, to dairy farmers who have been directed since January 1, 1964 . . . to remove their milk . . . from commercial markets because of residues of chemicals registered and approved for use by the Federal Government at the time of such use. The Secretary is also authorized to make indemnity payments for milk, or cows producing such milk, at a fair market value to any dairy farmer who is directed to remove his milk from commercial markets because of **(1) the presence of products of nuclear radiation or fallout if such contamination is not due to the fault of the farmer.** . . .

Emphasis added.

I don't have any actual statistics on the number of nuclear-armed dairy farmers, but I'd think it's pretty low. Maybe the concern is that farmers will forget to hose down their cows after somebody else's fallout cloud passes over, but it still seems like a stretch to call that kind of contamination their "fault."

7 U.S.C. § 450j (emphasis added).

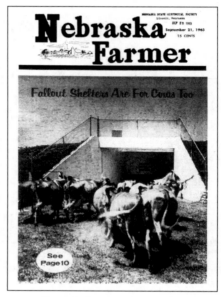

Fallout shelters are for cows, too.
Or at least they were in 1963.

You may be a member of the "unorganized militia" of the United States.

Under federal law going back at least 200 years, if you are a male citizen, 17 to 44 years old, you are likely a member of the "militia" whether you know it (or like it) or not:

Militia: composition and classes

(a) The militia of the United States consists of all able-bodied males at least 17 years of age and [with certain exceptions] under 45 years of age who are, or who have made a declaration of intention to become, citizens of the United States and of female citizens of the United States who are members of the National Guard.

(b) The classes of the militia are—

(1) the organized militia, which consists of the National Guard and the Naval Militia; and

(2) the unorganized militia, which consists of the members of the militia who are not members of the National Guard or the Naval Militia.

That is, those who fit the definition are in the unorganized militia unless they join the *organized* militia, so there's really no getting out of the militia. There are exceptions, of course, like if you are the vice president. You're probably not, though.

So what does this mean? Well, for one thing, under chapter 15 of the same title, if there is an insurrection or rebellion, the president can call up the militia — including the unorganized militia — to the extent he considers it necessary to suppress the uprising. That's hardly likely to be necessary, given that we now have, for better or worse, a standing army *and* the National Guard *and* super-heavily armed local police forces that could be used to suppress such things, but it is legally possible.

All 50 states have similar laws, so that's at least two clubs of which you may automatically be a member. Congratulations!

10 U.S.C. §§ 311–12, 331–34.

One who knowingly packs apples in any unapproved barrel shall pay a $1 penalty.

There are zillions of federal laws and regulations that have to do with standard measures used in commerce. The ones pertaining to apple barrels were passed in 1912 and might need to be updated, at least if we continue to have problems with nonstandard apple barrels:

> Any person, firm, or corporation, or association who shall knowingly pack or cause to be packed apples in barrels, or who shall knowingly sell or offer for sale such barrels in violation of the provisions of this Act shall be liable to a penalty of $1 and costs for each such barrel so sold or offered for sale, to be recovered at the suit of the United States in any court of the United States having jurisdiction.

For apple-packers who were previously unaware of this law and don't have a dollar to spare:

> The standard barrel for apples shall be of the following dimensions when measured without distention of its parts: Length of stave, twenty-eight and one-half inches; diameter of head, seventeen and one-eighth inches; distance between heads, twenty-six inches; circumference of bulge, sixty-four inches outside measurement, representing as nearly as possible seven thousand

and fifty-six cubic inches: Provided, That steel barrels containing the interior dimensions provided for in this section shall be construed as a compliance therewith.

Arguably, the Standard Apple Barrel Act of 1912 was superseded by the Standard Barrel Act of 1916, but the provisions above remain on the books. To avoid any risk of incurring a one-dollar-per-barrel penalty, therefore, you are still advised to adjust any noncompliant bulge circumferences with all deliberate speed.

15 U.S.C. §§ 231–33.

One good thing about losing an arm: you can legally use a switchblade.

It's illegal to make, sell, distribute, or possess a switchblade under federal law, except for soldiers or people with only one arm:

> Sections 1242 and 1243 of this title shall not apply to—
> (1) any common carrier or contract carrier, with respect to any switchblade knife shipped, transported, or delivered for shipment in interstate commerce in the ordinary course of business;
> (2) the manufacture, sale, transportation, distribution, possession, or introduction into interstate commerce, of switchblade knives pursuant to contract with the Armed Forces;
> (3) the Armed Forces or any member or employee thereof acting in the performance of his duty;
> (4) the possession, and transportation upon his person, of any switchblade knife with a blade three inches or less in length **by any individual who has only one arm;** . . .

If you lose the other arm, too, I guess it'll be illegal again. So be extra careful.

15 U.S.C. §§ 1242–44 (emphasis added).

U.S. jurisdiction over space vehicles is based on the status of the doors.

This makes some sense, I suppose, but it's at least interesting that jurisdiction over a U.S. space vehicle and, I guess, things that may happen within it, could come down to whether the doors are open or closed:

> The term "special maritime and territorial jurisdiction of the United States," as used in this title, includes:
>
> * * *
>
> (6) Any vehicle used or designed for flight or navigation in space and on the registry of the United States pursuant to the Treaty on Principles Governing the Activities of States in the Exploration and Use of Outer Space, Including the Moon and Other Celestial Bodies and the Convention on Registration of Objects Launched into Outer Space, while that vehicle is in flight, which is from the moment when all external doors are closed on Earth following embarkation until the moment when one such door is opened on Earth for disembarkation or in the case of a forced landing, until the competent authorities take over the responsibility for the vehicle and for persons and property aboard.

I guess this means that if Neil Armstrong had punched Buzz Aldrin, and Buzz had wanted to press charges, a U.S. court would have had jurisdiction over that dispute as long as it happened before they got back and opened the door (depending on where they landed). And because I know you're now wondering, what if they got in a fight on the Moon, I will tell you the answer would be the same, because the U.S. also asserts jurisdiction in "any place outside the jurisdiction of any nation with respect to an offense by or against a national of the United States."

Strangely enough, so far it seems no court has yet had the opportunity to construe these laws, but if you don't want your case to be the first, don't commit any outer-space crimes.

18 U.S.C. § 7.

It's legal to mail a live scorpion.

Most live animals, including poisonous insects and spiders, are "non-mailable." There is one exception—this one:

The U.S. Postal Service will, happily or not, carry this monster to its ultimate destination.

The Postal Service is authorized and directed to permit the transmission in the mails, under regulations to be prescribed by it, of live scorpions which are to be used for purposes of medical research or for the manufacture of antivenom. Such regulations shall include such provisions with respect to the packaging of such live scorpions for transmission in the mails as the Postal Service deems necessary or desirable. . . .

You may be happy to know there won't be any scorpions on a plane:

Nothing contained in this paragraph shall be construed to authorize the transmission in the mails of live scorpions by means of aircraft engaged in the carriage of passengers for compensation or hire.

And here's how you pack one:

Live scorpion is packed in a double container system, with each receptacle closed or fastened in such a way as to prevent escape.

Inner receptacle is made of material that cannot be punctured by a scorpion.

Inner receptacle is marked "Live Scorpion."

Cushioning material is used to prevent shifting of the inner receptacle.

Design of packaging is of sufficient strength . . . to prevent crushing of the mailpiece or escape of the contents during normal Postal Service handling and transport.

Address side of mailpiece is clearly marked "Live Scorpion."

These rules are important *because you are mailing somebody a live scorpion.*

18 U.S.C. § 1716(c); USPS Pub. 52, ex. 526.5
(Restrictions on Mailing Live Scorpions).[13]

A tax deduction is available for certain charitable donations of properly preserved dead animals.

Section 170 of the Internal Revenue Code contains specific rules about how to value charitable donations of "taxidermy property," which is just what you think it is:

> For purposes of this section, the term "taxidermy property" means any work of art which—
> (i) is the reproduction or preservation of an animal, in whole or in part,
> (ii) is prepared, stuffed, or mounted for purposes of recreating one or more characteristics of such animal, and
> (iii) contains a part of the body of the dead animal.

Wow, thanks for your kind donation, said no one.

Anyway, you must deduct from the taxidermy-donation deduction the appropriate amount of capital gains:

> [I]n the case of a charitable contribution . . . of any taxidermy property which is contributed by the person who prepared, stuffed, or mounted the property or by any person who paid or incurred the cost of such preparation, stuffing, or mounting, . . . the amount of gain which would have been long-term

capital gain if the property contributed had been sold by the taxpayer at its fair market value (determined at the time of such contribution).

Unless you are the taxidermist or the one who paid him:

[I]n the case of a charitable contribution of taxidermy property which is made by the person who prepared, stuffed, or mounted the property or by any person who paid or incurred the cost of such preparation, stuffing, or mounting, only the cost of the preparing, stuffing, or mounting shall be included in the basis of such property.

Congratulations to whoever represented the taxidermy industry on this one.

26 U.S.C. §§ 170(e)(1)(B)(iv) & 170(f)(15).

Certain whaling captains are entitled to deduct up to $10,000 per year from federal taxes.

This is the second of two highly specific deductions that are written into Section 170. To be clear, I have no problem with whaling captains or offering them a tax break. I guess I do think it signals some issues with the tax code in general if there is a need for a specific statutory provision allowing a deduction for certain "expenses paid by certain whaling captains in support of native Alaskan subsistence whaling" involving the taking of bowhead whales as regulated by the federal government pursuant to the Whaling Act of 1949 and managed by the Alaska Eskimo Whaling Commission:

> (1) In general.
> In the case of an individual who is recognized by the Alaska Eskimo Whaling Commission as a whaling captain charged with the responsibility of maintaining and carrying out sanctioned whaling activities and who engages in such activities during the taxable year, the amount described in paragraph (2) (to the extent such amount does not exceed $10,000 for the taxable year) shall be treated . . . as a charitable contribution.

(2) Amount described.
  (A) In general. The amount described in this paragraph is the aggregate of the reasonable and necessary whaling expenses paid by the taxpayer during the taxable year in carrying out sanctioned whaling activities.
  (B) Whaling expenses. [Defined to include boats, gear, food, storage and distribution, basically.]

(3) Sanctioned whaling activities.
For purposes of this subsection, the term "sanctioned whaling activities" means subsistence bowhead whale hunting activities conducted pursuant to the management plan of the Alaska Eskimo Whaling Commission.

Because we are talking about people engaged in subsistence hunting, meaning they are out on the Arctic Ocean hunting whales partly to make ends meet, I'm not sure how often a tax deduction would be useful to them. But if they need it, I'm all for it.

26 U.S.C. § 170(n).

You can't patent an atomic weapon.

Any citizen looking to join the nuclear club should know that, no matter how much better your bomb design is than the ones we have now, the federal government will still not let you patent it:

> No patent shall hereafter be granted for any invention or discovery which is useful solely in the utilization of special nuclear material or atomic energy in an atomic weapon.

And just in case anyone is unclear these days on what "atomic weapon" means, a definition is provided:

> The term "atomic weapon" means any device utilizing atomic energy, exclusive of the means for transporting or propelling the device (where such means is a separable and divisible part of the device), the principal purpose of which is for use as, or for development of, a weapon, a weapon prototype, or a weapon test device.

Basically, that defines "atomic weapon" as "an atomic-energy device that is a weapon," which itself is not too helpful. But it does include the phrase "principal purpose," and in a 1980 case that was helpful to a guy who had invented a special "fuel pellet configuration for laser fusion burn." The patent examiner denied his application, citing this law and saying the "principal purpose" of such pellets was in atomic weapons.

That's true, but the court decided that the word "solely" in the first sentence above was more important.

That is, patents will be denied only for inventions that are useful *solely* in atomic weapons. So if you come up with something that might also be useful in the kitchen, let's say, then go for it.

42 U.S.C. § 2181(a); 42 U.S.C. § 2014(d).

"Yep, that's a good one, Dan, but you're gonna need to come up with some practical use for it."

If you see an island covered in dung, you may legally claim it for the United States.

You may not seize such an island that already belongs to someone else, but if it doesn't, it's your lucky day:

> Whenever any citizen of the United States discovers a deposit of guano on any island, rock, or key, not within the lawful jurisdiction of any other government, and not occupied by the citizens of any other government, and takes peaceable possession thereof, and occupies the same, such island, rock, or key may, at the discretion of the President, be considered as appertaining to the United States.

This was—and still is—authorized by the Guano Islands Act of 1856, a law meant to help secure America's critical strategic dung reserves. ("Guano" is a more polite term for bat or bird dung.) There were no artificial fertilizers at the time and so guano, which is full of nitrates and phosphates in addition to God knows what else, was extremely valuable for that purpose. In fact, President Millard Fillmore considered the guano issue important enough that he mentioned it in his first State of the Union address in 1850.

Should he maybe have spent a little more time trying to head off the Civil War instead of worrying about national poop supplies? Scholars generally say yes.

In any event, the 1856 law authorized citizens to claim guano islands and extended U.S. jurisdiction over them once claimed. Guano hunters and dung miners then went to work.

One of the islands they grabbed was Navassa Island, two square miles of crap between Cuba, Jamaica, and Haiti. (Haiti also claims it, but good luck with that, Haiti.) Dung was mined there from 1865 until 1889, when workers rebelled and killed several supervisors. (Apparently digging and hauling dung in fierce tropical heat was not the most pleasant of jobs.) A worker named Jones was charged with murder, and he argued that he could not be prosecuted because the Guano Islands Act was unconstitutional.[14] It wasn't, and he was.

48 U.S.C. §§ 1411–19 (Chapter 8: Guano Islands).[15]

George Washington is technically the highest-ranking U.S. general ever.

Technically, of course, he is also dead, so it really doesn't matter. But it is true that in 1976, for the country's bicentennial, he was posthumously promoted to "General of the Armies of the United States" and declared to outrank everybody else, forever:

> Whereas Lieutenant General Washington of Virginia [did a whole bunch of stuff and was generally awesome]; and;
>
> Whereas it is considered fitting and proper that no officer of the United States Army should outrank Lieutenant General George Washington on the Army list: Now, therefore, be it
>
> Resolved by the Senate and House of Representatives of the United States of America in Congress assembled, That
>
> (a) for purposes of subsection (b) of this section only, the grade of General of the Armies of the United States is established, such grade to have rank and precedence over all other grades of the Army, past or present.
>
> (b) The President is authorized and requested to appoint George Washington posthumously to the grade of General of the Armies of the United States, such appointment to take effect on July 4, 1976.

President Ford then did that.

Washington's highest formal rank was lieutenant general, the equivalent of a three-star rank. Since then there have been lots of three- and four- and even five-star generals. Those guys may have had more stars but not more authority: Washington was also the commander-in-chief (and probably could have been king had he felt like it). So this seems like a case of "star inflation," not of people being promoted above him. But the 1976 law seems to make pretty clear that he is to be considered Numero Uno, past or present, perpetually.

H.J. Res. 519; Pub. L. No. 94-479 (Oct. 11, 1976).[16]

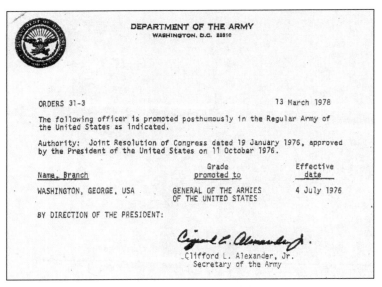

George Washington: permanently awesome

PART FOUR

The Laws of the States of the United States

Alabama's official state insect is a butterfly. It also has an official state butterfly. Which is also an insect.

When Alabama decided it wanted to have an official insect—and who wouldn't—it chose wisely:

> **State insect.**
> The monarch butterfly is hereby named and designated as the official insect for the State of Alabama.

So it seems a little odd that when it decided it also wanted an official *butterfly*, it didn't pick the one it already had:

> **State butterfly.**
> The Eastern Tiger Swallowtail is hereby designated as the official mascot and butterfly of the State of Alabama.

Originally I believed that in the rush to name an official butterfly, nobody bothered to check whether they already had one. On closer inspection, I noticed that both laws were passed at about the same time during the same legislative session, so it seems unlikely the sponsors of one were unaware of the other. But the legislature was apparently unable either to choose which insect/butterfly it preferred or to simply recognize two insect/butterflies as the official insect/butterflies of Alabama. The end result is that Alabama has an official insect that is a butterfly and an official butterfly that (like all butterflies) is also an insect.

The Eastern Tiger Swallowtail was also named the "official mascot," though, so who the hell knows.

ALA. CODE §§ 1-2-23, 1-2-24.

It's illegal to maim yourself in Alabama, but only for certain reasons.

Apparently Alabama has or once had a significant number of people who were willing to maim themselves rather than perform some "legal duty," or in order to increase their begging income:

> Maiming one's self to escape duty or obtain alms.
>
> Every person who, with design to disable himself from performing a legal duty, existing or anticipated, shall inflict upon himself an injury whereby he is so disabled and every person who shall so injure himself with intent to avail himself of such injury to excite sympathy or to obtain alms or some charitable relief shall be guilty of a felony.

What "anticipated legal duty" might prompt someone to maim himself rather than perform it? Well, generally people don't like jury duty, but they don't hate it *that* much. The only one that comes to mind is being drafted to serve in the armed forces—somebody might feel they are likely to get maimed or killed anyway if they go, so why not just cut to the chase and pre-maim themselves?

It really doesn't seem like an anti-maiming law would deter somebody who has already decided to self-maim, but there it is.

ALA. CODE § 13A-14-1.

Confederate widows, if any, would still be entitled to a pension.

At this point, it is *highly* unlikely anyone's going to make a claim, but if there were any Confederate widows left they would still be entitled to a pension under Alabama law:

> The widow of any person who actually served as a soldier or sailor in the army or navy of the Confederate States of America or of the State of Alabama for or during the period of the War Between the States, who was married to such soldier or sailor prior to January 1, 1904, or was married to such soldier or sailor for at least one year prior to the time of his death, regardless of whether his death occurred before or after September 23, 1919, and who has not remarried, except as provided in Section 31-8-3, and who was not at the time of her husband's death separated from him by divorce or was not voluntarily living apart from her husband during the period of one year prior to his death, and whose husband did not desert the service of the State of Alabama or the Confederate states, and who is an actual bona fide resident of Alabama and has been such for a period of five years prior to the filing of the application, and the widow of any Confederate soldier or sailor on the pension roll at the time of his death, shall be entitled to relief under the provisions of this chapter.

According to an Associated Press story, the last Civil War widow was Alberta Martin, who died in Alabama in 2004 at the age of 97. She married veteran William Jasper Martin in 1927 when she was 21 and he was 81. (When he died four years later, she married his grandson.) There was some dispute over whether she was entitled to a pension, but the state awarded her benefits in 1996. Another dispute erupted after the 1998 publication of Tony Horwitz's book *Confederates in the Attic*, which stated that William Martin had been a deserter. Under the statute, that would technically have disqualified his widow from receiving a pension—something no one wanted to see happen, and she continued to receive it.

It would not be mathematically impossible for another one to turn up. The last verified Confederate veteran was the outstandingly named Pleasant Crump, also from Alabama, who died in 1951. His second wife had died in 1942, but had he then managed to get himself an 18-year-old like William Martin did, let's say in 1950, she would still be only in her early 80s. So maybe Alabama shouldn't take this one off the books just yet.

According to *U.S. News and World Report*, as of July 2013 the federal government was still paying pension benefits to one child of a Civil War veteran.

ALA. CODE § 31-8-2.[17]

Billiard rooms can't have any secret passages.

At least if they connect to gambling dens or other immoral places:

> It shall be unlawful for any billiard room to maintain, or permit to be maintained, any open or secret connections, through doors, windows or trapdoors, panels, stairways, or other devices within any place where gambling is conducted or where persons congregate for immoral purposes.

Passed in 1923, presumably this law was aimed at preventing billiard rooms from being used as a "front" for hidden gambling or drinking activities, which were frowned upon at the time. Frankly, a billiard room doesn't seem like the smartest place to try to hide such things. Isn't that one of the first places they'd look? Were no churches available?

Setting that aside, it's not clear to me that this infringement on the fundamental right of all Americans to keep the government out of their secret passages is really justified. Unless there's actually something illegal going on at the other end, what has the passage owner done wrong? If there is something, punish the owner for hiding it. If there isn't, then get your agents out of his passage.

Maybe billiard-room operators were claiming to be shocked—shocked!—to learn what was going on at the other end of their secret passage, but let them tell that story and we'll let the jury decide.

ALA. CODE § 34-6-7.

The machines of Alaska
may not be deceived.

It may not fit the traditional definition of "theft," but it is illegal to obtain something from someone through deception (similar to fraud). In Alaska, it is no defense that the person you deceived was mechanical:

> In a prosecution under this chapter [Offenses Against Property] for an offense that requires "deception" as an element, it is not a defense that the defendant deceived or attempted to deceive a machine. For purposes of this section, "machine" includes a vending machine, computer, turnstile, or automated teller machine.

You know, if you have only *attempted* to deceive a turnstile, meaning that you failed, you should really be ashamed of yourself.

ALASKA STAT. § 11.46.985.

In Alaska, mooning someone is automatically "disorderly conduct."

It might be considered "disorderly" in other states, but I'm not sure that any others have listed mooning specifically:

A person commits the crime of disorderly conduct if,

(1) with intent to disturb the peace and privacy of another not physically on the same premises or with reckless disregard that the conduct is having that effect after being informed that it is having that effect, the person makes unreasonably loud noise;

(2) in a public place or in a private place of another without consent [and otherwise as stated above], the person makes unreasonably loud noise;

(3) in a public place, when a crime has occurred, the person refuses to comply with a lawful order of a peace officer to disperse;

(4) in a private place, the person refuses to comply with an order of a peace officer to leave premises in which the person has neither a right of possession nor the express invitation to remain of a person having a right of possession;

(5) in a public or private place, the person challenges another to fight or engages in fighting other than in self-defense;

(6) the person recklessly creates a hazardous condition for others by an act which has no legal justification or excuse; or

(7) the offender intentionally exposes the offender's buttock or
anus to another with reckless disregard for the offensive or
insulting effect the act may have on that person.

The other interesting point here is that "buttock" is singular. Is it
still "mooning" if only one is displayed? If so, then a full moon might
lead to two separate charges. No court has considered this specific
issue yet, so for now we can only speculate.

ALASKA STAT. § 11.61.110(a) (emphasis added).

But Alaska is more tolerant of rioters than other states are.

Most states have a law against "rioting," which means they have to define "riot." One thing everyone seems to agree on is that it takes more than one person to riot. No matter how hard you try, you can't "riot" by yourself. You can do lots of loud, dangerous, stupid things, but if you're the only one doing them that's still not a "riot," it's just you being a jerk.

What if another guy joins in? Personally, I'd say that's still just a pair of jerks, but some states, like California, will accept a riot of two:

> Any use of force or violence, disturbing the public peace, or any threat to use force or violence, if accompanied by immediate power of execution, by two or more persons acting together, and without authority of law, is a riot.

Most people, though, would probably agree that you need a minimum of three people for a group activity, and many states define riots accordingly. But not in Alaska, where it takes *six* to riot:

> A person commits the crime of riot if, while participating with five or more others, the person engages in tumultuous and violent conduct in a public place and thereby causes, or creates a substantial risk of causing, damage to property or physical injury to a person.

I imagine that groups of any significant size are rare enough in Alaska that they felt safe limiting the definition of "riot" to six or more (the main rioter plus at least five friends). The obvious lesson is that anybody with two to four friends who wants to be tumultuous should do it in Alaska.

In the United Kingdom, it actually takes *12* people to have a riot. A riot of more than 500 people, on the other hand, is legally defined as a "soccer match."

ALASKA STAT. § 11.61.100; CAL. PENAL CODE § 404(a).[18]

In Arizona, it is technically illegal to knowingly shine a flashlight on a peace officer.

The legislature was obviously concerned about laser beams, which can blind someone, but for some reason its definition of "laser pointer" is not limited to lasers:

> 13-1213. Aiming a laser pointer at a peace officer; classification; definition
>
> A. A person commits [the crime of] aiming a laser pointer at a peace officer if the person intentionally or knowingly directs the beam of light from an operating laser pointer at another person and the person knows or reasonably should know that the other person is a peace officer.
>
> B. Aiming a laser pointer at a peace officer is a class 1 misdemeanor.
>
> C. For the purposes of this section, "laser pointer" means any device that consists of a high or low powered visible light beam used for aiming, targeting or pointing out features.

A laser beam is especially dangerous because it's made up of coherent light and so its energy is very highly concentrated; it's not just a really bright light. And lasers do not necessarily lase in the visible spectrum, although of course the kind that are used in laser pointers (and as weapon sights) do. The point being that paragraph C is broad enough to apply to a flashlight, which after all is also a "low powered visible light beam" device used for "pointing out features."

We could probably trust most judges not to find somebody guilty of knowingly using a flashlight to point out a peace officer, but these days you never know.

ARIZ. REV. STAT. § 13-1213.[19]

Three states have official state neckwear.

They are Arizona, New Mexico, and Texas. Arizona and New Mexico accomplished this with very simple statutes:

- The Bola tie shall be the official state neckwear [of Arizona].
- The bolo tie is adopted as the official tie of New Mexico.

Obviously, they disagree on how to spell the name of the item and whether to capitalize it, but whatever. Texas, though, made a much bigger deal out of it:

WHEREAS, The State of Texas has customarily recognized a variety of official symbols as tangible representations of the state's culture and natural history; and

WHEREAS, The heritage of the Lone Star State is closely associated with images of cowboys and the western frontier, and these elements inform several of the current Texas symbols, including rodeo, the official state sport, and the longhorn, the state large mammal; and

WHEREAS, A singular fashion associated with the American West is the bolo tie, also known as the bola tie, which is distinguished by its decorative clasp that fastens a length of cord or string; a staple of the western-wear fashions sported by a large number of Texans, the bolo tie conjures up the romance of the pioneer era and speaks to the determination and independence that figure so prominently in Lone Star lore; and

[three more "whereas" clauses omitted]

WHEREAS, The bolo tie symbolizes both the state's iconic western culture and the originality of its residents, and it is indeed appropriate that this handsome and unique apparel receive special legislative recognition; now, therefore, be it

RESOLVED, That the 80th Legislature of the State of Texas hereby designate the bolo tie as the official State Tie of Texas.

But as you will see later on, this is by no means the dumbest resolution to ever make it through the Texas House.

ARIZ. REV. STAT. §§ 41-857; N.M. STAT. 12-3-4; Tex. H.R. Con. Res. No. 12, 80th Leg., Reg. Sess. (2007).[20]

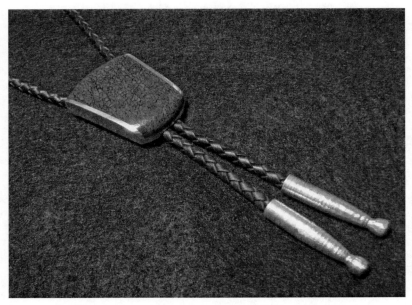

This "handsome and unique apparel": the bolo and/or bola tie.

Arizona has an official state butterfly, which it would like to make clear is not protected.

The same statute that makes the Two-Tailed Swallowtail the official state butterfly of Arizona also declares:

> Designation of the state butterfly pursuant to this section shall not constitute grounds for protection of the butterfly or its habitat.

Apparently the Arizona legislature wanted to make sure you knew that it likes the Two-Tailed Swallowtail but doesn't like it all that much.

Ariz. Rev. Stat. §§ 41-860.

There's an official pronunciation of "Arkansas."

Confusion about this had apparently arisen by 1881, when the General Assembly first passed a resolution addressing the matter:

> Whereas, confusion of practice has arisen in the pronunciation of the name of our state and it is deemed important that the true pronunciation should be determined for use in oral official proceedings.
>
> And, whereas, the matter has been thoroughly investigated by the State Historical Society and the Eclectic Society of Little Rock, which have agreed upon the correct pronunciation as derived from history and the early usage of the American immigrants.
>
> Be it therefore resolved by both houses of the General Assembly, that the only true pronunciation of the name of the state, in the opinion of this body, is that received by the French from the native Indians and committed to writing in the French word representing the sound. It should be pronounced in three (3) syllables, with the final "s" silent, the "a" in each syllable with the Italian sound, and the accent on the first and last syllables. The pronunciation with the accent on the second syllable with the sound of "a" in "man" and the sounding of the terminal "s" is an innovation to be discouraged.

That is, it's "AR-kan-saw," not "Ar-KAN-sus."

The resolution was made binding law and codified in 2011. There is no official penalty for saying it incorrectly, but I'd be willing to bet that an unofficial penalty would be imposed almost immediately on anybody who said "Ar-KAN-sus" within Arkansas.

Note, however, that this is only the law with regard to the State of Arkansas and geographical features located within it. If you are speaking of, for example, Arkansas City, Kansas (a town near that state's border with Oklahoma), the proper pronunciation is "Ar-KAN-sus City." The name of the Arkansas River, which flows through all these states plus Colorado, is often pronounced differently depending on which state it happens to be in at the time. And since most of you will probably never visit any state in this region during your entire lives, I think we can probably leave it at that.

ARK. CODE § 1-4-105; Ark. H.R. Con. Res. No. 4, Acts 1881, p. 216.

There's also an official possessive form of "Arkansas."

It's not clear how long *this* debate may have been going on, but it was (more or less) resolved in 2007:

> WHEREAS, confusion has arisen concerning the appropriate spelling of the possessive form of the name of our state; and
>
> WHEREAS, it is deemed important that the correct spelling of the possessive form of Arkansas be used in official documents and publications; and
>
> WHEREAS, the matter has been thoroughly investigated and the agreed Possessive form . . . is "Arkansas's"; and
>
> WHEREAS, there is precedent for addressing such matters by means of a concurrent resolution of the General Assembly, such as in Concurrent Resolution 4 of 1881, which established the correct pronunciation of the name of our state and which was later incorporated into the Arkansas Code in 1987 as § 1-4-105,
>
> NOW THEREFORE, BE IT RESOLVED BY THE HOUSE OF REPRESENTATIVES OF THE EIGHTY-SIXTH GENERAL ASSEMBLY OF THE STATE OF ARKANSAS, THE SENATE CONCURRING THEREIN:
>
> That the General Assembly hereby determines that the correct spelling of the possessive form of the name of our state is "Arkansas's".

BE IT FURTHER RESOLVED that this resolution shall be considered to be supplemental to Concurrent Resolution 4 of 1881, which established the correct pronunciation of the name of our state.

You might use this in a sentence such as "Arkansas's legislature has nothing better to do."

Ark. H.R. Con. Res. 1016 (2007).

Hijacking and carjacking are technically known as "vehicular piracy."

The word "hijacking" is commonly associated with airplane travel, but it works perfectly well with other vehicles too. These days the word "carjacking" is used more often in that context, but not in Arkansas.

> A person commits vehicular piracy if, without lawful authority, the person seizes or exercises control, by force or threat of violence, over any:
> (1) Aircraft occupied by an unconsenting person; or
> (2) Other vehicle:
> (A) Having a seating capacity of more than eight (8) passengers;
> (B) Operated by a common carrier or contract carrier of passengers for hire; and
> (C) Occupied by an unconsenting person.

Seizing a vehicle with a smaller seating capacity is known as "stealing," unless one or more unconsenting persons are inside, in which case it's also known as "kidnapping."

Seizing a vehicle that appears to have a *much* smaller seating capacity but somehow turns out to have a couple dozen clowns in it is not considered a crime at all, as long as you drive them out of the state.

ARK. CODE § 5-11-105.

In California, comic books must be less than 80 percent mayhem.

Or at least if they contain 80 percent mayhem or more, sellers can't be forced to carry them.

A law originally passed in the 1950s, when comics were deemed second only to communism in terms of the level of threat to American values, defines "horror comic books" as those in which:

> the commission or attempted commission of the crime of arson, assault with caustic chemicals, assault with a deadly weapon, burglary, kidnapping, mayhem, murder, rape, robbery, theft, or voluntary manslaughter is set forth by means of a series of five or more drawings or photographs in sequence. . . .

A ban would have violated the First Amendment, so the legislature settled for a law that made it a crime for wholesalers to pressure unwilling sellers into carrying the horror comics.

The definition, though, seems to torpedo the whole thing. Four horrific scenes in a row are apparently okay, and as long as every fifth scene is nonhorrific, there's no problem. Basically, California has limited horror comics to 79.9 percent mayhem, although how that helps is not entirely clear.

CAL. BUS. & PROF. CODE § 16603.[21]

A California real-estate agent must tell a buyer if someone has recently died on the property.

"*Should* tell a buyer" might be more accurate, because the statute doesn't specifically require this disclosure. But the immunity it gives a seller or real-estate agent for *failing* to make this disclosure applies only if the death was more than three years before the date of the buyer's offer:

> No cause of action arises against an owner of real property or his or her agent, or any agent of a transferee of real property, for the failure to disclose to the transferee the occurrence of an occupant's death upon the real property or the manner of death where the death has occurred more than three years prior to the date the transferee offers to purchase, lease, or rent the real property. . . .
>
> Nothing in this section shall be construed to immunize an owner or his or her agent from making an intentional misrepresentation in response to a direct inquiry . . . concerning deaths on the real property.

If they ask, you have to tell the truth, but you aren't required by this statute to volunteer the fact of any death that happened there more than three years before.

But you should, because in 1983 a court held that a woman could sue a seller and agent because they didn't tell her five people had been killed in the house 10 years before.[22] One could argue—and the defendants did—that whether she was afraid of ghosts or just creeped out, she was being irrational, and a seller's duty of disclosure should not be based on irrational concerns. But the court decided that she should get a chance to prove that the house was worth less than she thought—because, for example, future buyers might *also* irrationally want to avoid the place.

The statute above was passed in response to this case. The three-year limit seems pretty arbitrary, but then I guess it's as good as any. The upshot is that if the death was more than three years ago, you don't need to volunteer it. Otherwise, you need to disclose it, although you probably don't need to put it in the brochure.

CAL. CIV. CODE § 1710.2.[23]

Superfluity does not vitiate.

For those who may have been puzzling over questions related to superfluity, California's Civil Code answers at least one of them:

> Superfluity does not vitiate.

Good to know?

Since "superfluous" means unnecessary, redundant, or surplus, and "vitiate" means to spoil, impair, weaken, debase, or make invalid, this seems to mean that just because you have more of something than you need doesn't mean the first one is somehow irrelevant. Is that helpful?

It shows up remarkably often in case law, although I suspect that's because judges' clerks have some kind of contest going. In one case, it was used to defeat an argument that because the legislature had passed two identical statutes, when it later repealed one of them it was actually repealing both.[24] I guess if you have a legislature that accidentally passes identical statutes, this would come in handy. But for the most part, it seems, well, superfluous.

The part of the Code in which the superfluity thing appears is a list of "maxims of jurisprudence," basically rules of interpretation you might use to support or oppose a position if you don't have a *good* argument. They are "intended not to qualify" other Code provisions, "but to aid in their just application." Okay, but I'm not sure these offer much aid.

Some of them are just not true:

> The law never requires impossibilities.
>> The law neither does nor requires idle acts.
>> The law disregards trifles.

Whoever came up with those has obviously never practiced law.
Others might be good for philosophy class, but it's hard to see how you would use them in real life:

> That which ought to have been done is to be regarded as done. . . .
> That which does not appear to exist is to be regarded as if it did not exist.
> That is certain which can be made certain.
> Things happen according to the ordinary course of nature and the ordinary habits of life.
> A thing continues to exist as long as is usual with things of that nature.

Yep, things happen, and then they hang around as long as those things usually do. Very helpful, thanks.

I'll admit that this one might come in really handy, if anyone paid attention to these things:

> The law has been obeyed.

CAL. CIV. CODE §§ 3509–3548.

The law pertaining to frog-jumping contests.

A 1957 California law provides an exception to the rules that would normally govern frog-taking *if* the frog or frogs are taken for the purpose of competing in a frog-jumping contest:

> As used in this article, "frog-jumping contest" means a contest generally and popularly known as a frog-jumping contest which is open to the public and is advertised or announced in a newspaper.
>
> Frogs to be used in frog-jumping contests shall be governed by this article only. Frogs to be so used may be taken at any time and without a license or permit.
>
> If the means used for taking such frogs can, as normally used, seriously injure the frog, it shall be conclusively presumed the taking is not for the purposes of a frog-jumping contest.
>
> Any person may possess any number of live frogs to use in frog-jumping contests, but if such a frog dies or is killed, it must be destroyed as soon as possible, and may not be eaten or otherwise used for any purpose.
>
> A frog which is not kept in a manner which is reasonable to preserve its life is not within the coverage of this article.

The idea of a frog-jumping contest was popularized in Mark Twain's 1865 short story, "The Celebrated Jumping Frog of Calaveras County." Calaveras County is in California, and it does have a yearly frog-jumping contest, but the story came first.

Generally, it's against the law in California to "take, possess, sell, transport or export frogs for human consumption," with limited exceptions that require a permit. The statutes above are obviously intended to encourage frog-jumping contests but also to prevent people who just want to eat frogs from using such a contest as an excuse.

CAL. FISH & GAME CODE §§ 6880–6885.

If you manage to kill a great white shark in self-defense, you still have to throw it back.

Surely this can't happen very often, and if it did happen, it would seem fair to make an exception:

(a) It is unlawful to take any white shark (Carcharodon carcharias) for commercial purposes [unless you have a permit]. . . .

(b) Notwithstanding subdivision (a), white sharks may be taken incidentally by commercial fishing operations using set gill nets, drift gill nets, or roundhaul nets. . . . White sharks taken pursuant to this subdivision, if landed alive, may be sold for scientific or live display purposes.

(c) Any white shark killed or injured by any person in self-defense may not be landed.

I wouldn't want to keep it, but in the unlikely event that I am actually able to kill a great white shark in self-defense, I'm sure as hell gonna land it so I can tell everybody in earshot that I did that. Fine me if you want, but I'm not letting that one go unnoticed.

CAL. FISH & GAME CODE § 8599.

One may not soak a rabbit carcass for more than two and a half hours, tops.

According to a website that I looked at for about 10 seconds before getting totally creeped out, you are in fact supposed to soak a rabbit carcass in cold, salty water for a while after you slaughter and (I think) skin it. There was probably a reason. Apparently, though, in the 1960s some people in California were going overboard with this:

> It is unlawful for any person to immerse or soak the carcass of any slaughtered rabbit in water for a period longer than necessary to eliminate the natural animal heat in the carcass and in no event for a period longer than 2 1/2 hours.

As you can see, two and a half hours is the absolute max for rabbit-soaking. Could be five minutes if for some reason the rabbit you got was a little short on natural animal heat, or up to 150 minutes if you got yourself a hot one. It all depends.

CAL. FOOD & AGRIC. CODE § 26991.

Nor shall one make false egg proclamations.

Fraud and slander are against the law anyway, so it's not clear why California law has a special statute that prohibits the making of any false or deceptive statement about eggs, by any means, including "public outcry or proclamation." But it does:

> It is unlawful for any person to make any statement, representation, or assertion orally, by public outcry, or proclamation, or in writing, or by any other manner or means whatever concerning the quality, size, weight, condition, source, origin, or any other matter relating to eggs which is false, deceptive, or misleading in any particular.

The statute is obviously intended to be all-inclusive ("by any . . . manner or means whatever"), so the laundry list preceding that statement really isn't necessary. But I enjoy imagining that the legislature acted because somebody was going around loudly making wild accusations about the nature of someone's eggs.

No one should have to put up with that.

CAL. FOOD & AGRIC. CODE § 27637.

California's official state animal has been extinct since 1922.

Hard to say exactly what the significance of any official state animal really is, but if yours is extinct, that doesn't seem to send the message you might be hoping for:

> The state animal is the California Grizzly Bear (Ursus Californicus) as depicted in outline, details, and in colors on the official representation in the custody of the Secretary of State. The color references of the bear shall be in accordance with those set forth in Section 420.
>
> All state representations of the state animal in details and in colors shall be in accordance with this section and shall correspond substantially with the following representation thereof:
> [embarrassingly poor representation of grizzly bear omitted]

According to the California Department of Parks and Recreation, the Californians who revolted against the Mexican government in June of 1846 chose the grizzly bear as the symbol for their movement (and one of the symbols on the flag of the California Republic) "because of its strength and unyielding resistance."

According to the California State Library, the last California grizzly bear was killed in Tulare County in August 1922.

CAL. GOV. CODE § 425.[25]

Something about huckleberry.

I *think* this says it's illegal in California to mess with plants you don't own:

Every person who within the State of California willfully or negligently cuts, destroys, mutilates, or removes any tree or shrub, or fern or herb or bulb or cactus or flower, or huckleberry or redwood greens, or portion of any tree or shrub, or fern or herb or bulb or cactus or flower, or huckleberry or redwood greens, growing upon state or county highway rights-of-way, or who removes leaf mold thereon, except that the provisions of this section shall not be construed to apply to any employee of the state or of any political subdivision thereof engaged in work upon any state, county, or public road or highway while performing work under the supervision of the state or of any political subdivision thereof, and every person who willfully or negligently cuts, destroys, mutilates, or removes any tree or shrub, or fern or herb or bulb or cactus or flower, or huckleberry or redwood greens, or portions of any tree or shrub, or fern or herb or bulb or cactus or flower, or huckleberry or redwood greens, growing upon public land or upon land not his or her own, or leaf mold on the surface of public land, or upon land not his or her own, without a written permit from the owner of the land signed by the owner or the owner's authorized agent, and every person who knowingly sells, offers, or exposes for sale, or transports for sale, any tree or shrub, or fern or herb or bulb or cactus or flower, or huckleberry or redwood greens, or portion of any tree or shrub, or fern or herb or bulb or cactus or flower, or huckleberry or redwood greens, or leaf mold, so cut or removed from state or county highway rights-of-way, or removed from public land or from land not owned by the person who cut or removed the same without the written permit from the owner of the land, signed by the owner or the owner's authorized agent, is guilty of a misdemeanor and upon conviction thereof shall be punished by a fine of not more than one thousand dollars ($1,000), by imprisonment in a county jail for not more than six months, or by both fine and imprisonment.

So don't do that.

CAL. PENAL CODE § 384a.

In California, you could be convicted of participating in your own lynching.

While the common understanding of a "lynching" is shaped by the fact that many of them end in murder, technically a "lynching" occurs as soon as two or more people remove a person from the lawful custody of the authorities. Or as California law defines it:

> The taking by means of a riot [which, remember, takes at least two people in California] of any person from the lawful custody of any peace officer is a lynching.
>
> Every person who participates in any lynching is punishable by imprisonment pursuant to subdivision (h) of Section 1170 for two, three or four years.

Again, this has frequently been done to inflict illegal, extrajudicial punishment, but under this definition the punishment is not part of the lynching itself. And that is why a guy in California was convicted of his own lynching.[26]

In that case, Anthony J. had been arrested and handcuffed by police, but "he struggled with them and repeatedly yelled for assistance to a crowd that eventually swelled to 200 or 300 people. After being handcuffed, Anthony continued his attempts to break away and his appeals for assistance from the crowd. The crowd finally charged the officers and pulled Anthony away. He fled, still handcuffed, and eluded capture."

After he was recaptured, he was tried and convicted of several charges, including lynching. He appealed on the grounds that the law was intended to *protect* people from being lynched, "and therefore cannot be violated by a person who is the subject of the lynching." He probably thought that sounded like a pretty good argument, because it does.

But despite the "commonly understood connotations of 'lynching,'" the court held, the statutes were broader than that. Anthony had "participated" in the riot that ultimately freed him, and because "every person who participates in any lynching is punishable," Anthony went to jail for lynching himself.

CAL. PENAL CODE §§ 405a, 405b.[27]

It's legal to break into a house to make an arrest— and also to break back out again if it goes badly.

There really is such a thing as a citizen's arrest, but as these two old California statutes suggest, you might want to leave the arresting to the police, at least if it would require you to break into a house to nab the suspect.

It's legal to do that if you are after a felon, but notice that you are required to ask first:

> To make an arrest, a private person, if the offense is a felony, and in all cases a peace officer, may break open the door or window of the house in which the person to be arrested is, or in which they have reasonable grounds for believing the person to be, after having demanded admittance and explained the purpose for which admittance is desired.

But felons are frequently dangerous people, so that it is not at all impossible that the person you are trying to nab could turn the tables on you. (Especially if you asked to come in first, thus warning him you were coming.) But California has thought of that, so it also made it legal for you to break back *out*:

Any person who has lawfully entered a house for the purpose of making an arrest, may break open the door or window thereof if detained therein, **when necessary for the purpose of liberating himself,** and an officer may do the same, when necessary for the purpose of liberating a person who, acting in his aid, lawfully entered for the purpose of making an arrest, and is detained therein.

I doubt anyone would be too upset with you for breaking out if you really had to, but they might think you were kind of a bonehead for breaking in there in the first place.

Cal. Penal Code §§ 844–45 (emphasis added).

California is wise to your "not-a-U-turn-but-a-series-of-smaller-turns-with-the-same-result" defense.

I'm not saying that I've ever actually carried out an illegal U-turn, but one who had might well have justified it to himself at the time by thinking that what he was doing did not technically violate the law because it was not a continuous movement in the shape of a "U," but rather a succession of several different and entirely independent movements or turns that, when completed, just happened to have the same end result as a single U-turn would have had, had it been carried out in a continuous fashion.

Anyone who thought that, in California at least, would have been wrong:

> A "U-turn" is the turning of a vehicle upon a highway so as to proceed in the opposite direction whether accomplished by one continuous movement or not.

This is one of those cases where you can infer from the statute that somebody has probably run this argument up the flagpole at least once before after being caught making a U-turn.

That somebody was not me. I'm just pointing this out.

CAL. VEH. CODE § 665.5.

The boundaries of Colorado aren't the ones described in its constitution.

Colorado's state constitution says this:

> The boundaries of the state of Colorado shall be as follows: Commencing on the thirty-seventh parallel of north latitude, where the twenty-fifth meridian of longitude west from Washington crosses the same; thence north, on said meridian, to the forty-first parallel of north latitude; thence along said parallel, west, to the thirty-second meridian of longitude west from Washington; thence south, on said meridian, to the thirty-seventh parallel of north latitude; thence along said thirty-seventh parallel of north latitude to the place of beginning.

The thirty-seventh parallel, therefore, is the boundary between Colorado and New Mexico.

Only it isn't.

More than one state has found out that its state lines are not where they're supposed to be. Surveyors in the 1800s didn't have GPS, and they did their best but the lines are not always accurate. In 1868, Congress hired somebody to survey the boundary between what were then the New Mexico and Colorado Territories, and he did, and maps were made, and life went on.

In 1902, another survey showed his line was actually south of the parallel, but moving it north then would have meant transferring "a large strip of territory from Colorado to New Mexico, including the greater portions of one town and two villages, and five post offices."[28] New Mexico decided it wanted those, and in 1919 it sued. In 1925 the Supreme Court ruled that regardless of which survey was right—and "it may well be that neither is entirely correct"—everybody should stick with the line they'd been using for 50 years.

New Mexico's constitution is also wrong, by the way.

Colo. Const. art. I.

In Colorado, an officeholder is technically required to give "personal attention" to his or her duties.

Colorado's state constitution also says this:

> Section 2. Personal attention required
>
> No person shall hold any office or employment of trust or profit, under the laws of the state or any ordinance of any municipality therein, without devoting his personal attention to the duties of the same.

Irritating, if you took office with the understanding that you would be able to benefit from that office without actually having to do anything. On the other hand, it does not appear that anyone has ever been removed from office for this reason.

During World War II, someone argued that the district attorney for Pueblo County should be removed from office because he had enlisted in the U.S. Army and, Pueblo County not being in any particular danger at the time, he had been sent elsewhere. The Colorado Supreme Court didn't fault him for that, noting that his deputies were handling things just fine and county administrators had voted to keep paying him during his service in the armed forces. Understandable, but there's no question that the state constitution was violated unless he was prosecuting people by mail from overseas.

A more interesting case was decided in 1902, when a judge named Owers was accused of not devoting his personal attention to his office in Leadville because he was frequently gone "for health reasons." He took office in 1895, but starting in 1897 he claimed that health problems had left him unable to sleep at high altitude. (Leadville is almost a mile higher than Denver, which is itself a mile high.) He thereafter spent most of his time in Denver except for five months in Santa Barbara, California ("which place is on the sea coast," the court noted).

The plaintiff was clearly suspicious of this zero-altitude, beachfront excuse, but the court bought it.

Colo. Const. art. XII, § 2.[29]

No nuclear bomb can be set off in Colorado unless the voters approve it.

Probably the intent here was to prevent any nuclear testing in Colorado, but if the federal government found it necessary to test there, a state constitutional provision couldn't stop it from doing so as long as the test was on federal land. (Hopefully a very large chunk of it.) And as drafted, the provision seems to preclude any nuclear detonations, regardless of who's doing the detonating, unless the detonating party has first obtained consent from the people of Colorado:

Section 1. Nuclear detonations prohibited - exceptions
No nuclear explosive device may be detonated or placed in the ground for the purpose of detonation in this state except in accordance with this article.

Section 2. Election required
Before the emplacement of any nuclear explosive device in the ground in this state, the detonation of that device shall first have been approved by the voters through enactment of an initiated or referred measure authorizing that detonation, such measure having been ordered, proposed, submitted to the voters, and approved as provided in section 1 of article V of this constitution.

Section 2 refers only to underground testing, but Section 1 is broader: "No nuclear explosive device may be detonated . . . in this state except in accordance with this article."

Maybe this is an ingenious defense plan, intended to protect Colorado by forcing anybody who wants to attack it to go through the process of getting an initiative passed first, which might be more difficult and expensive than building a bomb. Any potential terrorist or other attacker would be discouraged by this and call off the attack. Or maybe it would just attack a neighboring state that hasn't thought of this yet. Either way works, if you're Colorado.

As we will see, anti-nuke laws of one kind or another are pretty common, but this is the only one to my knowledge requiring that the detonation be put to a vote.

Colo. Const. art. XXVI, §§ 1–2.

In Connecticut, you can't hunt squirrels with dynamite.

Well, you *can*, and it might actually be pretty effective. It's just not legal:

> **Use of explosives.** No person shall take or attempt to take any gray squirrel, rabbit or other fur-bearing animal protected by law by the use of gunpowder, dynamite or other explosive compound, or by fire, smoke, brimstone, sulphur, gas or chemical, or by digging from any hole or den, provided nothing herein shall be construed to prevent the shooting of any gray squirrel or rabbit or fur-bearing animal. Any person who violates any provision of this section shall be guilty of a class C misdemeanor.

You can see how the authorities would be reluctant to let people use weapons of mass destruction to go after individual critters, or possibly to clean out their dens, just because of the danger of overkill (literally). What's surprising about the statute is that presumably it was necessary because people were actually waging war against fur-bearing animals this way.

More surprising, maybe, is the prohibition on fire and brimstone. "Brimstone" is an old word for sulfur, which has been used for ages as a pesticide, hence the Biblical references (about a dozen of them) to "fire and brimstone" as things one might rain on someone or something that had displeased one, if one were a deity.[30] That word has not been commonly used for a long time, though, and the statute specifically lists sulfur anyway. "Brimstone" must be referring to something else, but what?

It is tempting to think the law is intended to forbid "fire and brimstone" sermons as an attempt to pray the rabbits out of the ground, but that would probably violate the First Amendment.

CONN. GEN. STAT. § 26-88.

Connecticut does not consider the Boy Scouts to be a "private military force."

This is not the same as the "militia," which as noted earlier in connection with federal law technically includes (usually) all male citizens who are 17 to 44 years old. The concern here is about people who set up on their own for potential military purposes. Any such group must register and, not coincidentally, provide a roster of its members.

This particular law was passed in 1949, at a time when the state was probably concerned about communists. The legislators did want to make clear, though, that they were not concerned about potential armed rebellions by (for example) the Boy Scouts or the Catholic Boys Brigade:

> "Private military force" . . . includes any group of five or more persons organized or associated together in a camp, group, organization, company, association or society, or in any other manner, for the purpose of drilling or maneuvering with firearms or other dangerous weapons, or with imitations, copies or replicas thereof, or for the purpose of giving or acquiring military training or experience; but said term "private military force" shall not include any military or police units of the United States or of any state or territory, or of any political subdivision of any state or territory, . . . or any society or fraternal organization which features a uniform or costume with side-arms or replicas thereof for display purposes only, or The Boy Scouts of Amer-

ica, The Catholic Boys Brigade of the United States, Inc., or troops of a foreign government whose admission to the United States has been consented to by the federal or state government, or any person acting or appearing in any theater, motion picture or television production while actually engaged in representing therein military or naval characters or scenes.

Do the Boy Scouts "drill or maneuver with firearms" or otherwise provide "military training"? Unless there's a merit badge for insurrection that I don't know about, I'm not sure why anyone would have thought the Boy Scouts needed a specific exception.

CONN. GEN. STAT. §§ 27-101, 27-102.[31]

On the other hand, those spears look pretty sharp.

If you gather up seaweed or manure, you can keep it if you take it home within 24 hours.

If you've always wanted your own clump of seaweed, Connecticut will let you have some under these conditions:

> **Marine vegetable deposits**. No right in any marine vegetable deposit, thrown up by the sea or by a navigable river, shall be acquired by any person by his gathering it together upon any public beach, unless he removes it within twenty-four hours thereafter.

It is a fairly ancient rule that one who mixes labor with unowned property—let's say he goes to a public beach and rakes up some piles of a "marine vegetable deposit," also known as "seaweed"—may then be considered to own that property. In Connecticut, the law says that you lose any such right unless you remove the piles within 24 hours. That's why Mr. Church lost in *Church v. Meeker*, an 1867 case before the state supreme court. Church "heaped up the weed," as the court put it, but didn't remove it for a day or two. Meeker happened along in the meantime and took all that good weed for himself. The court held Meeker was justified because Church had waited too long.

But by the same token, the act of heaping does create a property right that lasts 24 hours. This was confirmed a few years later in *Haslem v. Lockwood*, when the same court awarded heaps of abandoned horse manure to the guy who had raked it up in the first place. Everybody agreed the manure originally belonged to the owners of the horses that produced it, but they had clearly "abandoned" it on the highway. The heaper argued he had made the abandoned manure his property by virtue of creating the heaps, while the finder argued, in part, that the heaper had re-abandoned it by leaving the heaps there overnight. Referring to the seaweed statute, the court held that the heaper had done a public service by raking up the manure, and that the rights he gained in it thereby should last at least 24 hours.

This rule applies only to seaweed or manure that has been, let's say, "deposited" on public land, so don't try to rake up somebody else's private manure and then claim it as your own.

CONN. GEN. STAT. § 50-8.[32]

Those finding an item worth more than $1 must file a police report.

These laws, passed in the 1940s, are still on the books in Connecticut. They were a little odd to begin with and obviously have not been adjusted for inflation:

Duties of finder. Any person who finds and takes possession of any article of the value of one dollar or more shall report the finding of such article to the police department of the municipality in which he finds such article within forty-eight hours from the time of such finding. The finder of such article shall, at the time of reporting, furnish to the police department the date, time and place of finding, his name and address and a description of the article found, and, within a period of one week from such finding, shall deliver such article to the police department. Any person who violates or fails to comply with the provisions of this section shall be guilty of a class D misdemeanor.

Advertising; sale of perishable goods. The police department shall, commencing within one week from the date of receipt of any lost article, advertise a general description of such article once a week for at least two successive weeks in a newspaper having a circulation in such municipality and shall retain custody of such article for six months from the date of receipt thereof, unless it is claimed by the rightful owner within such six months' period. The requirement of advertising may be omitted when the value or estimated value of the article is less than two dollars. Perishable or obnoxious property or articles of a dangerous or harmful nature may be sold or otherwise disposed of as soon as practicable on the best terms available.

One dollar in 1949 would be worth about $10 today, so this seems like a lot of paperwork for items that most people would not bother to track down if lost. The cost of advertising would be more than some items are worth.

I'd be concerned if I lost any "obnoxious property," but on the other hand I might not want to be seen picking it up.

CONN. GEN. STAT. §§ 50-10, 50-1.

"Punt guns" are no longer permitted in Delaware.

The "punt gun" was typically fired from either a small boat or the shoulder of one's summer intern.

Wikipedia describes a "punt gun" as "a type of extremely large shotgun," and as you can see it's hard to argue with that description. Because of its size, it was not exactly practical to use in everyday life, unless you had a friend to rest it on, a special punt-gunning hat and a large number of people you didn't like who would hold still while you pointed a giant shotgun at them. Instead, these were generally mounted on small boats, or "punts," and used to hunt waterfowl. In other words, it was a super-giant shotgun for those who wanted to kill multiple birds at once.

Sadly, in Delaware you now have to kill one at a time:

> No person shall shoot at, or kill any bird or animal protected by the laws of this State with any device, swivel or punt gun, or with any gun other than such as is habitually raised at arm's length and fired from the shoulder [your own shoulder]. Possession of such illegal device or gun while hunting shall be prima facie evidence of an offense under this subsection.

The same section restricts the use of muzzle-loading rifles to "primitive weapon season," and muzzle-loading smoothbore weapons don't appear to be allowed at all, except for a single-shot muzzle-loading pistol "to provide the coup-de-grace, if required." These items along with bows and arrows are the only weapons with which one may hunt deer.

It's not clear to me whether you could hunt other kinds of animals with spears or perhaps your teeth and claws alone, so before attempting something like this during primitive weapon season, you should consult a primitive Delaware lawyer.

DEL. CODE ANN. tit. 7 § 704(d).

Feel free to do your worst to a woodchuck.

States protect some animals and not others, and then there are some they just really don't like. In Delaware, the woodchuck (a.k.a. groundhog) falls into that last category.

> The animal known as woodchuck or groundhog shall not be a form of protected wildlife in this State.

Actually, that might be understating things a bit. Just in case anyone was still unclear on the status of this animal, the legislature added this next:

> The woodchuck or groundhog may be hunted, trapped, caught, shot, killed, sold, shipped or otherwise disposed of, by any person and at any time.

Then they added this one:

> The woodchuck or groundhog may also be taunted, mocked, or humiliated prior to its demise, which if at all possible should be an extended and painful one in accordance with its status as the most heinous of vermin.

Okay, I made that one up, but it was probably in the first version of the bill.

DEL. CODE ANN. tit. 7 §§ 797–98.

It's illegal to tell people about marriage in any state other than Delaware.

This is called "advertising marriage in another state," which, for some reason, Delaware doesn't want you to do:

> A person is guilty of advertising marriage in another state when the person erects any sign or billboard, or publishes or distributes any material giving information relative to the performance of marriage in another state.
>
> Advertising marriage in another state is a violation. In addition, a peace officer of this State may seize and destroy any sign, billboard or material which the officer observes in violation of this section.

It's in the same part of the code as bigamy, and just after a statute that precludes leaving Delaware to "contract a bigamous marriage" and then coming back. So it could be that the purpose is to prevent the latter, but regardless it's hard to see this being constitutional.

Del. Code Ann. tit. 11 § 1004.

The oath-swearing provisions in Delaware were first enacted in 1852, and they look it.

§ 5321. Method of administering.
The usual oath in this State shall be by swearing upon the Holy Evangels of Almighty God. The person to whom an oath is administered shall lay his or her right hand upon the book.

Not too different than in other states so far.

§ 5322. Uplifted hand.
A person may be permitted to swear with the uplifted hand; that is to say, a person shall lift up his or her right hand and swear by the ever living God, the searcher of all hearts, that etc., and at the end of the oath shall say, "as I shall answer to God at the Great Day."

That's something you might have seen a lot of in 1852, but not so much today. Even then, though, they did allow for the fact that not everyone might be comfortable with the above:

§ 5323. Affirmation.
A person conscientiously scrupulous of taking an oath may be permitted, instead of swearing, solemnly, sincerely and truly to declare and affirm to the truth of the matters to be testified.

Although you also get the sense that in 1852 they were not all that comfortable with non-Christians:

§ 5324. Non-Christians.
A person believing in any other than the Christian religion, may be sworn according to the peculiar ceremonies of such person's religion, if there be any such.

That probably wasn't meant the way it sounds, but still.

DEL. CODE ANN. tit. 10 §§ 5321–24.

The "tongue-splitting" regulations, on the other hand, are much more recent.

Here it's not so much the law that is weird as the race of beings to which it applies. Some members of that race apparently have *asked* to have their tongues surgically altered to be "forked or multi-tipped":

(a) A person is guilty of tongue-splitting in the first degree if the person is neither a physician nor a dentist, holding a valid license issued under the laws of the State of Delaware, and the person performs an act of tongue-splitting on any other person in this State. Tongue-splitting in the first degree is a class A misdemeanor.

(b) A doctor or dentist is guilty of tongue splitting in the second degree if the doctor or dentist performs an act of tongue-splitting in this State and the person on whom the act of tongue-splitting is performed is either:

    (1) Under the influence of alcohol or a controlled substance; or

    (2) Is a minor and the person has failed to obtain the prior written and notarized consent of the minor's adult parent or legal guardian to the specific act of tongue-splitting.

Tongue-splitting in the second degree is a class B misdemeanor.

***

(g) For the purposes of this section "tongue-splitting" means the surgical procedure of cutting a human tongue into 2 or more parts giving it a forked or multi-tipped appearance.

To give Delaware some credit here, it has addressed a thoroughly creepy fringe practice not by banning it, which never works anyway, but rather by regulating it to make sure that the person asking for it is old enough and sober enough to make a rational decision to have his or her tongue split and, you know what, I guess it wouldn't bother me too much if they just banned this outright.

DEL. CODE ANN. tit. 11 § 1114A.

No puppet shows without a license.

I imagine that the ban on unlicensed puppet shows in private homes is very rarely enforced, but the fact remains that performing such a show "in any house" would technically be illegal in Delaware:

§ 901. License for shows and other exhibitions.

(a) Whoever for money or other reward in any city or town in this State exhibits any images or pageantry, sleight of hand, tricks, puppet shows, circus, any feats of balancing, personal agility, strength or dexterity, or any theatrical exhibition, without a license first obtained as provided in this section shall forfeit and pay to the city or town a fine as set by the city or town.

(b) The mayor of any city, the commissioners of any town, or if there are no commissioners, any justice of the peace residing in or nearest to such town, may grant a license for such exhibitions on receiving for the use of the city or town such sum as they deem proper, not less than $5.00, for every such exhibition.

(c) Whoever wilfully suffers any unlicensed exhibition to be had or made in any house or upon any premises in his possession shall pay to the city or town a fine as set by the city or town.

(d) This section does not extend to any permanently established museum, nor to any merely literary, scientific or musical exhibition.

Some constitutional problems immediately jump to mind, such as the ban on exhibiting "images or pageantry" without first asking officials for a license. That is a classic "prior restraint" of the kind that is very likely to violate the First Amendment.

Also, the Fourth Amendment should protect someone's right to do any of this stuff inside his own home, although the government could probably ban in-home circuses.

DEL. CODE ANN. tit. 28 § 901.

In Florida, it's illegal to molest a manatee.

This would be illegal anywhere in the United States because manatees are an endangered species protected by federal as well as state law. But the species that lives in the United States doesn't range very far outside of Florida, so we might as well focus on that state's anti-manatee-harassment law:

(2) PROTECTION OF MANATEES OR SEA COWS.—

(a) This subsection shall be known and may be cited as the "Florida Manatee Sanctuary Act."

(b) The State of Florida is hereby declared to be a refuge and sanctuary for the manatee, the "Florida state marine mammal." The protections extended to and authorized on behalf of the manatee by this act are independent of, and therefore are not contingent upon, its status as a state or federal listed species. . . .

(d) Except as may be authorized by the terms of a valid state permit issued pursuant to paragraph (c) or by the terms of a valid federal permit, it is unlawful for any person at any time, by any means, or in any manner intentionally or negligently to annoy, molest, harass, or disturb or attempt to molest, harass, or disturb any manatee; injure or harm or attempt to injure or harm any manatee; capture or collect or attempt to capture or collect any manatee; pursue, hunt, wound, or kill or attempt to pursue, hunt, wound, or kill any manatee; or possess, literally or constructively, any manatee or any part of any manatee.

Do people actually do these things to poor, harmless manatees? Well, I don't know how you tell when a manatee is "annoyed," but people do harass, disturb, and (technically) molest them. In 2012, a woman was arrested for trying to ride one, and in May of that year two boneheads were arrested because one had filmed the other doing a "cannonball" onto a manatee (and then posted the evidence on YouTube).

Manatees have enough trouble without humans jumping on them, so please refrain.

FLA. STAT. § 379.2431(2).

It's still legal to take a picture of a farm without written consent. At least for now.

In 2011, a Florida state senator introduced a bill that would have made it a crime to take a picture of a farm or similar property without the owner's written consent. The penalty for this heinous crime? Up to 30 years in prison:

> A person who photographs, video records, or otherwise produces images or pictorial records, digital or otherwise, at or of a farm or other property where legitimate agriculture operations are being conducted without the written consent of the owner, or an authorized representative of the owner, commits a felony of the first degree. . . .

The bill was aimed at animal-rights groups who investigated corporate farms with hidden cameras, but it was written so broadly that it would have been a felony for a tourist to take an unauthorized picture of a farm from a passing car. Classifying the crime as a first-degree felony meant that in Florida, taking an unauthorized picture of a farm would have been a more serious crime than manslaughter.

A committee analysis of the bill did note "potential First Amendment issues with the bill as written because the bill does not require that the offender actually be on private property to be guilty of photographing" that property. The bill was later amended to fix that problem, and the offense was also reduced to a misdemeanor, someone apparently having recognized that farm photography was really not in the same class as homicide.

The amended bill actually passed the Florida Senate 25–10; it then went to the Florida House of Representatives, where it quietly died.

Fla. S.B. 1246, §§ 2, 3 (filed Feb. 21, 2011).[33]

In Georgia, you can't sell kids under 12 to a clown.

You also can't rent them, or even give them away for free. How's a clown supposed to get himself an indentured servant these days?

> Any person who shall sell, apprentice, give away, let out, or otherwise dispose of any minor under 12 years of age to any person for the vocation, occupation, or service of rope or wire walking, begging, or as a gymnast, contortionist, circus rider, acrobat, or clown, or for any indecent, obscene, or immoral exhibition, practice, or purpose shall be guilty of a misdemeanor.

On the other hand, it's only a misdemeanor.

GA. CODE ANN. § 39-2-17.

You also can't steal human body parts from an accident scene.

You *are* allowed to take them, briefly, but only for certain specified purposes:

> It shall be unlawful for any person to remove from the scene of the death or dismemberment of any person any human body part; provided, however, that this Code section shall not apply to a law enforcement officer acting in the lawful discharge of his or her official duties, or to any person acting under the direction of a law enforcement officer, a physician or an emergency medical technician in the course of their professions, or in the absence of any such person to any person who transports such body part directly to a medical facility, law enforcement agency, or licensed funeral home, although all such persons remain obligated to comply with the provisions of Article 2 of Chapter 16 of Title 45 concerning death investigations.
>
> Any person violating the provisions . . . of this Code section shall be guilty of a misdemeanor of a high and aggravated nature.

Too bad for whoever was out there looking for souvenirs or whatever the hell was going on, but good for the rest of humanity.

GA. CODE ANN. § 16-12-161.

It is legal to sell
squirrel tails.

There has been some confusion on this point, but it is in fact legal to sell squirrel tails in Georgia as long as the squirrel was taken (that is, killed) legally. The legislature passed a special statute just to clarify this important point:

> Notwithstanding any other provision of this title to the contrary, it shall be lawful to sell the tails of legally taken squirrels.

It's not all that easy to tell when and how you can actually take squirrels legally, though. Here are the rules:

→ Squirrels are off-limits from March 1 to August 14.
→ You can kill as many as you want between August 15 and February 29, as long as you don't kill more than 12 a day. This is a little confusing, because the law says there is no "bag limit," but the daily limit in fact effectively prevents you from killing more than 2,376 squirrels a year (or 2,388 in a leap year).
→ *Unless* you're a falconer:

> Notwithstanding the provisions of subsections (a) and (b) [above], it shall be unlawful to take the species designated below, except squirrels, by means of falconry at any time during the period March 16 through September 30; but it shall not be unlawful to take the species designated below, except squirrels, by means of falconry during the period October 1 through

March 15. It shall be unlawful to take squirrels by means of fal-
conry at any time during the period March 16 through August
14, but it shall not be unlawful to take squirrels by means of fal-
conry at any time during the period August 15 through March
15 in such number not exceeding the bag limits. . . .

So, if I understand this correctly, you can hunt squirrels from
August 15 to February 29, falcon or no falcon, but if you use falcons
you get an extra couple of weeks, which works out to a maximum of
2,556 squirrels per year if taking said squirrels at least in part by means
of falcon-assisted hunting.

If there are any squirrels left by then, anyway.

GA. CODE ANN. §§ 27-3-15(a)(9), 27-3-15(b)(9), 27-3-15(f), 27-3-23.

Benefit of clergy no longer exists.

This doesn't mean Georgia hates clergy, just that it has abolished the old common-law doctrine by that name:

> Since it is no longer needed or appropriate, the ancient device of benefit of clergy shall not exist.

"Benefit of clergy" originally referred to the fact that church officials were subject to a separate set of laws, or at least they argued they were when they were in trouble for something secular. And the King did grant them a limited immunity, mostly to make amends for what happened after he loudly "suggested" in the presence of guys with swords that he'd like to be "rid" of the troublesome Thomas Becket. So a churchman charged with a crime could invoke this "benefit of clergy" and put his case under church jurisdiction.

Not surprisingly, it appears that the number of "clergy" then skyrocketed, at least among criminal suspects. Back then it wasn't that easy to check out such a claim, and one way they tested it was to ask the suspect to read Psalm 51 out of the Bible. Very few laypeople could read at the time, so this was a reasonable idea.

Not surprisingly, it appears that the number of people who memorized Psalm 51 then skyrocketed. But by then, some concern was developing over the harshness of the justice system and its increasing use of the death penalty, which was *mandatory* for almost all felonies. "Benefit of clergy" was seen as one way out of this, and so in many cases they didn't check too closely whether somebody was actually looking at the words when he recited Psalm 51.

Eventually, they just dropped the pretext entirely, so that even lay-people could make a (one-time) claim of "benefit of clergy"—sort of like having a "Get Out of Jail Free" card. Did that really work? Yes. In fact, the two British soldiers convicted of manslaughter after the Boston Massacre invoked "benefit of clergy" to escape execution.

This was still part of the common law in 1789, though it was already declining, and in many states, like Georgia, it has been abolished by statute. In the others—well, it might or might not be worth giving it a shot.

GA. CODE ANN. § 16-3-27.[34]

You can't tattoo anyone within one inch of their eye socket.

Seems like a good idea, doesn't it?

> (a) As used in this Code section, the term "tattoo" means to mark or color the skin of any person by pricking in, inserting, or implanting pigments, except when performed by a physician licensed as such pursuant to Chapter 34 of Title 43.
>
> (b) It shall be unlawful for any person to tattoo the body of any person within any area within one inch of the nearest part of the eye socket of such person. Any person who violates this Code section shall be guilty of a misdemeanor.

This is one of those laws from which I think we can infer that (1) some people have actually asked to be tattooed within one inch of an eye socket and (2) that didn't go so well.

GA. CODE ANN. § 16-12-5.

No noodling or grabbling without a permit.

As is true in several other states, Georgia does allow both noodling and grabbling, although only as to flathead, channel, and blue catfish, and only between March 1 and July 15:

(a) It shall be unlawful to fish for game fish, catfish, and all other species of fish in the freshwaters of the state by grabbling, noodling, or hand grabbing except as provided in this Code section. Flathead, channel, and blue catfish may be taken by hand without the aid of any device, hook, snare, net, or other artificial instrument and without the aid of any scuba equipment, air hose, or other artificial breathing apparatus between March 1 and July 15 of each year.

(b) It shall be unlawful to alter any natural or manmade feature by placing boards, wire, barrels, buckets, or any device or obstruction in any stream or other body of water or to modify any log, hole, or other feature in an attempt to attract or capture fish by grabbling, noodling, or hand grabbing or to take fish by grabbling, noodling, or hand grabbing from such altered devices. It shall also be unlawful to raise any part of a natural or artificial device out of the water to aid in the hand capture of enclosed fish. . . .

(d) It shall be unlawful for any person to engage in the grabbling, noodling, or hand grabbing of flathead, channel, or blue catfish in the fresh waters of this state without a resident or non-resident fishing license as provided in Code Section 27-2-23.

What are "noodling" and "grabbling"? The statute provides a clue by also limiting what it refers to, redundantly, as "hand grabbing" — these are all ways to catch fish with your bare hands. Noodling and/or grabbling, however, are unique. They involve not just hand-grabbing a catfish, but actually flapping your hand around in a catfish hole until the fish tries to bite down on it, then jamming your hand into its mouth and yanking the whole fish up out of the water, probably with a shout of triumph followed by a guzzling of the PBR clutched in your other hand.

That last part is optional.

GA. CODE ANN. § 27-4-37.

It's also illegal to "lay drags."

This practice has many names, most likely, but in Georgia, it's officially known as "laying drags":

> (a) No driver of any motor vehicle shall operate the vehicle upon the public streets, highways, public or private driveways, airport runways, or parking lots in such a manner as to create a danger to persons or property by intentionally and unnecessarily causing the vehicle to move in a zigzag or circular course or to gyrate or spin around, except to avoid a collision or injury or damage.
>
> (b) The offenses described in this Code section shall be sufficiently identified on any traffic ticket, warrant, accusation, or indictment when referred to as "laying drags."
>
> (c) This Code section shall not apply to drivers operating vehicles in or on any raceway, drag strip, or similar place customarily and lawfully used for such purposes.
>
> (d) Any person violating subsection (a) of this Code section shall be guilty of a misdemeanor.

It seems unlikely that NASCAR drivers were getting tickets for "intentionally causing a vehicle to move in a circular course," but subsection (c) is there to protect them just in case.

GA. CODE ANN. § 40-6-251.

There are laws that apply to ski resorts, but Georgia doesn't have any ski resorts.

The statute includes a definition of "ski area":

> "Ski area" means all snow ski slopes or trails and other places under the control of a ski area operator at a defined business location within this state.

Not a lot of snow in Georgia, and no ski areas at all.

The answer here is that Georgia did have at least one for a while, up in the Blue Ridge Mountains in the far north part of the state. Sky Valley Resort had five trails, two lifts, and a vertical drop of no less than 250 feet, but amazingly it doesn't seem to have been economically viable.

It does drop below freezing in the Blue Ridge Mountains in the winter at night, but the average snowfall in that area is only about one inch per year.

GA. CODE ANN. § 43-43A-1.

A pay toilet is not a "bona fide coin operated amusement machine."

You need to have a license in Georgia to have a location where "bona fide coin operated amusement machines" are available, and although you wouldn't think any great mysteries would arise as to the meaning of that phrase, the definition is somewhat elaborate:

> "Bona fide coin operated amusement machine" means:
>
> (A) Every machine of any kind or character used by the public to provide amusement or entertainment whose operation requires the payment of or the insertion of a coin, bill, other money, token, ticket, card, or similar object and the result of whose operation depends in whole or in part upon the skill of the player, whether or not it affords an award to a successful player pursuant to subsections (b) through (g) of Code Section 16-12-35, and which can be legally shipped interstate according to federal law[, and] [e]very machine of any kind or character used by the public to provide music whose operation requires the payment of or the insertion of a coin, bill, other money, token, ticket, or similar object such as jukeboxes or other similar types of music machines.

In case you still aren't sure, the statute contains a list of examples of "bona fide coin operated amusement machines," which include but are not limited to: pinball machines, video games, that thing with the crane, that thing with the claw, "kiddie ride games," trivia machines, and "laser games" (if any).

In case you're *still* puzzled, there is also a list of things that *aren't* "bona fide coin operated amusement machines," such as: washing machines, vending machines, pay telephones, parking meters, gas and electric meters, "coin operated massage beds" (an exclusion I would dispute), and maybe oddest of all, pay toilets.

If anyone has ever mistaken a pay toilet for a "coin operated amusement machine," bona fide or otherwise, I'd appreciate learning about that incident.

GA. CODE ANN. § 50-27-70.

You can't ride a motorcycle in your socks.

Again, here's one that's a good idea, but one that you'd also think people would be able to figure out without a law:

(a) A person operating a motorcycle shall ride only upon the permanent and regular seat attached thereto; and such operator shall not carry any other person nor shall any other person ride on a motorcycle unless such motorcycle is designed to carry more than one person, in which event a passenger may ride upon the permanent and regular seat if designed for two persons or upon another seat firmly attached to the motorcycle at the rear or side of the operator.

(b) A person shall ride upon a motorcycle only while sitting astride the seat, facing forward, with one leg on either side of the motorcycle.

(c) No person shall operate a motorcycle while carrying any package, bundle, or other article which prevents him from keeping both hands on the handlebars.

(d) No operator shall carry any person, nor shall any person ride, in a position that will interfere with the operation or control of the motorcycle or the view of the operator.

(e) No person shall operate or ride upon a motorcycle unless he shall wear some type of footwear in addition to or other than socks.

Given the apparent need to legislate how to ride a motorcycle in the first place, though—"only while sitting astride the seat, facing forward, with one leg on either side of the motorcycle"—I guess they figured they might as well throw in the bit about socks.

But since the law they came up with still makes it perfectly legal to ride while wearing flip-flops, sandals, high heels, or any other type of nonsock "footwear," it's not clear to me what this has actually achieved.

GA. CODE ANN. § 40-6-311.

In Hawaii, it's illegal to harbor a mongoose.

Hawaii is really not fond of the mongoose. It's not legal to keep one or even to "harbor" one that might be on the lam, unless you have a (rarely granted) mongoose permit:

> **Mongoose; keeping or breeding; penalty.** It shall be unlawful for any person to introduce, keep or breed any mongoose within the State except upon and according to the terms of a written permit which may be granted therefor by the department of agriculture, in its discretion, to scientists, scientific institutions, associations, or colleges, or to officers, boards, or commissions of the State or any county. The department shall not issue a permit authorizing the keeping or breeding of mongoose within either the county of Kauai or the island of Lanai. Any person who violates this section shall be fined not less than $250 nor more than $1,000 for each mongoose introduced, kept or bred contrary to this section.
>
> **Harboring mongoose; penalty.** Any person harboring, feeding, or in any way caring for a mongoose, except upon and according to the terms of a written permit . . . shall be penalized. . . .

The law dates back to 1892, although it has been amended several times. Just to make sure mongooses mongeese mongoose members of this species know they aren't welcome, the legislature added a section in 1986 that basically encourages people to kill any mongoose on sight:

Mongoose; killing allowed. No person shall be prohibited from killing a mongoose in any manner not prohibited by law, including by trapping.

The mongoose is not native to Hawaii—sugar cane farmers imported them and turned them loose in 1883 in order to control rats. They'd probably be really good at catching rats, except that rats are active at night and mongoose(s) are active during the day (something no one bothered to check, apparently) so the two species never really encountered each other. The mongoose has proven very effective at killing and eating native birds and the eggs of endangered turtles, however—things that no one wants it to do.

HAW. REV. STAT. §§ 142-92, 142-93, 142-93.5.[35]

Some mongoose delinquents hanging out on a street corner, hassling native species

You can take home all the driftwood you want, but only one gallon of sand per day.

Not surprisingly (it being made up of islands), Hawaii has many statutes that apply to the shoreline, reefs, submerged lands, and so forth. A couple of those concern the ability of beachcombers to take home certain things, including the beach:

> **Driftwood.** All wood of any description which may drift on to the beach of any part of the State shall be the property of the finder, and anyone finding such driftwood may take the same for the finder's own private use, without paying a share to the State; provided that this section shall not be construed to apply to any vessel wrecked or stranded on any part of the shores of the State.
>
> * * *
>
> **Prohibitions.** The mining or taking of sand, dead coral or coral rubble, rocks, soil, or other marine deposits seaward from the shoreline is prohibited [except for certain maintenance-related purposes or] the taking from seaward of the shoreline of such materials, not in excess of one gallon per person per day for reasonable, personal, noncommercial use. . . .

If you are consistently using one gallon of sand per day, though, you may need to seek help for problem scavenging anyway.

You may also need to take advantage of this exception while you can. In 2013, the legislature considered but did not pass a bill that would have put an end to the one-gallon allowance. Supporters noted that the state's beaches were already suffering from erosion, and to allow individuals to remove up to 365 gallons per year was not a good idea.

Should this become law, it does contain an exception for the *inadvertent* taking of sand such as may be "inadvertently carried away on the body and on clothes, toys, recreational equipment, and bags," so it's good to know they won't be criminalizing that.

Haw. Rev. Stat. §§ 7-2, 171-58.5.

You can't drop anything out of an airplane except water, sand, or "paper handbills."

A law dating back to 1923 makes "dangerous flying" illegal, and that includes dropping anything out of an airplane, with three exceptions:

> **263-9 Dangerous flying a misdemeanor; penalty.** Any aeronaut or passenger who, while in flight over a thickly inhabited area or over a public gathering within the State, engages in trick or acrobatic flying, or in any acrobatic feat, or flies, except while in landing or taking off, at such a low level as to endanger the persons on the surface beneath, or drops any object except loose water or loose sand ballast, or paper handbills, shall be guilty of a misdemeanor and punishable by a fine of not more than $1,000, or imprisonment for not more than one year, or both.

I'm not sure they would be too keen on flying around and unloading sand on people below, assuming anyone was in the habit of doing that kind of thing, but the law does seem to say that's okay. The law is old enough that it might be referring only to water or sand in the form of ballast of the kind used in balloons, so I wouldn't rely on this if you have any plans to dump sand on a bunch of Hawaiians.

Haw. Rev. Stat. § 263-9.

State employees still have to work on Buddha Day *and* Bodhi Day.

Hawaii has designated April 8 and December 8 as "Buddha Day" and "Bodhi Day" respectively, but has also made clear that these are not official state holidays:

> **Buddha Day**. April 8 of each year shall be known and designated as "Buddha Day", provided that this day is not and shall not be construed to be a state holiday.
>
> * * *
>
> **Bodhi Day**. December 8 of each year shall be known and designated as "Bodhi Day" in recognition that on this day Prince Siddhartha Gautama, after six years of study and rigorous ascetic practices and meditation, attained "enlightenment" or "awakening" to the true nature of existence, which was later conceptualized as the "Four Noble Truths." This day is not and shall not be construed to be a state holiday.

As I understand it, which is poorly, a "buddha" is one who has gained insight into the true nature of things (*the* Buddha obviously being one of these), and "bodhi" is the insight or knowledge that such a person has gained. I don't know why Buddha Day and Bodhi Day would be two different days, if the Buddha became a buddha on the day he attained bodhi, but this is just one of many things I don't know about both buddhas and bodhi.

I do know that Hawaii state employees don't get either day off.

Also recognized-but-not-state-holidays in Hawaii: Arbor Day, Lei Day, Respect for Our Elders Day, Kupuna Recognition Day, Makahiki Commemoration Day, Discoverers' Day (Polynesian discoverers only), Baha'i New Year's Day, Asian Lunar New Year Week of Commemoration in Hawaii, Queen Lili'uokalani Day, and Financial Literacy Month.

HAW. REV. STAT. §§ 8-1, 8-10.

Sorcery per se is no longer a crime in Hawaii.

According to a note in the current version of Hawaii's criminal code, Hawaii law previously criminalized both fortune-telling and "sorcery." Those laws were repealed, however, as had been suggested by the drafters of the Model Penal Code:

> Fortune telling has . . . been made an offense in some codes. Hawaii law previously had such a provision. Again, it is hard to see why this activity should be made a penal offense per se. If the activity amounts, under aggravated circumstances, to theft by deception, the theft sections can be employed. The argument in favor of making fortune telling an offense has been stated [as follows]:
>
> "There may be some question whether this conduct should continue to be criminal. However, persons holding themselves out to possess occult powers very often proceed to take advantage of the gullible and persuade them to turn over money or property. While this activity amounts to theft by deception [citing section], it may be difficult to prove. A prohibition against fortune telling, etc., as such drives the activity underground and reduces somewhat the opportunity to practice frauds."
>
> In view of the coverage by the offense of theft, the utility to be gained from driving the activity underground seems marginal. Indeed, driving the activity underground would reduce the opportunity to discover and prove theft by deception which arises in this context.

Hawaii law previously contained a section making sorcery an offense. Since the section is based on using pretended power to cure another, rather than intent to defraud that person, the practice seems adequately covered and penalized as practicing medicine without a license.

The motivation for the repeals, therefore, was to simplify the code. This also demonstrates that Hawaii is significantly more advanced than, say, Papua New Guinea, which (as discussed below) has only recently repealed its "Sorcery Act."

HAW. REV. STAT. § 708-881 (commentary).

In Idaho, cannibalism is against the law unless you can prove it was really necessary.

Idaho is the only state that has a specific law against cannibalism—not that other states try to encourage it—but even Idaho is willing to make an exception if you ate someone only because you had to:

> CANNIBALISM DEFINED—PUNISHMENT. (1) Any person who wilfully ingests the flesh or blood of a human being is guilty of cannibalism.
>
> (2) It shall be an affirmative defense to a violation of the provisions of this section that the action was taken under extreme life-threatening conditions as the only apparent means of survival.
>
> (3) Cannibalism is punishable by imprisonment in the state prison not exceeding fourteen (14) years.

The law helpfully defines the term, I guess in case someone isn't sure what "cannibalism" is and might engage in it by mistake.

Is this law necessary? No, it is not. So far as I can tell, cannibalism has not exactly been a rampant problem in Idaho, no matter how sick of potatoes people may get. It's not like people do this on a whim, and if someone does, that person has almost certainly committed some other crime for which he or she could be punished. This is probably why no other states have bothered with a specific law on this, even given the extreme creep factor.

It also seems unlikely that such a law would be helpful in deterring cannibalism. Anyone inclined to it normally is not likely to be thinking clearly anyway. And if people are in a situation involving "extreme life-threatening conditions" that might require this "as the only apparent means of survival," the pre-cannibalism debate is probably not going to involve a lengthy discussion of the legal issues involved.

IDAHO CODE ANN. § 18-5003.

In Illinois, consumers must be warned not to nuzzle a reptile.

The law requires any reptile-seller to post a notice regarding "safe reptile-handling practices" for the benefit of consumers interested in getting themselves a new cuddly little scaly friend:

> The notice regarding safe reptile-handling practices [shall contain] all of the following statements:
>
> (A) "As with many other animals, reptiles carry salmonella bacteria, which can make people sick. Safe reptile-handling steps should be taken to reduce the chance of infection."
>
> (B) "Always wash your hands thoroughly after you handle your pet reptile, its food, and anything it has touched."
>
> (C) "Keep your pet reptile and its equipment out of the kitchen or any area where food is prepared. Kitchen sinks should not be used to bathe reptiles or wash their dishes, cages, or aquariums. If a bathtub is used for these purposes, it should be cleaned thoroughly and disinfected with bleach."
>
> (D) "Don't nuzzle or kiss your pet reptile."
>
> (E) "Keep reptiles out of homes where there are children under 5 years of age or people with weakened immune systems. . . ."

(F) "Pet reptiles should not be allowed in child care centers."

(G) "Pet reptiles should not be allowed to roam freely throughout the home or living area."

Other than that, pet reptiles sound like lots of fun.

225 ILL. COMP. STAT. § 605/18.1.

They also must be warned not to wear bowling shoes outside.

The shoes are very slippery, you see:

> **Operator notice to bowlers.** An operator shall post a notice in a conspicuous place near each bowling center entrance and exit that reads as follows: "Bowling shoes are specialized footwear and are not intended to be worn outside a bowling center because the bowling shoes may be affected by substances or materials such as: snow, ice, rain, moisture, food, or debris. Such substances or materials on bowling shoes that have been worn outside a bowling center may cause the person wearing the bowling shoes to slip, trip, stumble, or fall on the floor or alley surfaces in the bowling center."
>
> **Civil liability.** If the operator posts a notice in a conspicuous place near each bowling center entrance and exit in the form described in Section 10, the operator, except for willful and wanton misconduct, shall not be held civilly liable for injuries resulting from a slip, trip, stumble, or fall inside the bowling center solely caused by some substance or material on the bowler's bowling shoes that was acquired outside the bowling center immediately before entering or re-entering the bowling center.

As you might guess from that second paragraph, the real purpose of the law is to give bowling alleys (which, it seems, have had an image upgrade to "bowling centers") an immunity from lawsuits that people have been filing after they go outside in slippery bowling shoes, fall, and hurt themselves. Presumably, legislators who were especially concerned about bowlers agreed to compromise by voting for immunity if the bill also required bowling centers to post a sign warning bowlers that they might "slip, trip, stumble, or fall" if they go outside in bowling shoes.

According to news reports, an increase in the number of falling bowlers, or at least of lawsuits by bowlers alleging that they fell, was an unintended consequence of a state ban on indoor smoking.

745 Ill. Comp. Stat. §§ 41/10, 41/15.

It's a felony to possess more than 37 lizards for commercial purposes.

This assumes that the fair market value of a lizard is not more than eight dollars at any given time, because this Illinois statute provides that the minimum value of a lizard shall not be less than "$8 per animal in whole or in part." You'll need to keep an eye on what lizards (or lizard parts) are worth, because possessing $300 worth of them for commercial purposes is a felony:

> Any person who, for profit or commercial purposes, knowingly captures or kills, possesses, offers for sale, sells, offers to barter, barters, offers to purchase, purchases, delivers for shipment, ships, exports, imports, causes to be shipped, exported, or imported, delivers for transportation, transports or causes to be transported, carries or causes to be carried, or receives for shipment, transportation, carriage, or export any aquatic life, in part or in whole of any of the species protected by this Code, . . . and that aquatic life, in whole or in part, is valued at or in excess of a total of $300, as per species value specified in subsection (c) of this Section, commits a Class 3 felony.
>
> * * *
>
> For purposes of this Section, the fair market value or replacement cost, whichever is greater, must be used to determine the value of the species protected by this Code, but in no case shall the minimum value of all aquatic life and their hybrids protected

by this Code, whether dressed or not dressed, be less than the
following: . . . (4) For frogs, toads, salamanders, lizards, and
snakes, $8 per animal in whole or in part.

If the fair market value of a lizard went up to $250, say, then you
could only have one. But if it dropped to $7, the statutory floor of $8
would still apply. Therefore, one could have a maximum of 37 lizards
and still be in compliance with the $300 limit. Note that for purposes
of the statute, any partial lizard shall be treated as if it were whole. This
provision seems to discriminate against those who deal in lizard parts,
but as far as I know that is not illegal.

You might still be able to argue that you didn't have all those lizards for commercial purposes, although if you have $600 worth on
you (that's a maximum of 74 lizards), that's presumed to be evidence
of commercial intent.

515 ILL. COMP. STAT. § 5/5-25.

In Indiana, fighting's illegal unless it is part of a carefully regulated sport *or* is totally unplanned and spontaneous.

Indiana has outlawed "combative fighting," also known as "extreme" or "toughman" fighting, but seems to have struggled with how to do that without also outlawing other sports in which people often get combative:

> (a) As used in this chapter, "combative fighting" (also known as "toughman fighting", "badman fighting", and "extreme fighting") means a match, contest, or exhibition that involves at least (2) contestants, with or without gloves or protective headgear, in which the contestants:
>> (1) use their:
>>> (A) hands;
>>> (B) feet; or
>>> (C) both hands and feet;
>> to strike each other; and
>> (2) compete for a financial prize or any item of pecuniary value.

Competing in or promoting such an event is illegal.

But, you may be asking, wouldn't that definition also cover sports like boxing, martial arts, pro wrestling, and maybe even hockey? Well, it would, except that:

> (b) The term does not include:
>> (1) a boxing, sparring, or unarmed combat match . . . . ;
>> (2) mixed martial arts . . . .;
>> (3) martial arts . . . .;
>> (4) professional wrestling . . . ; or
>> (5) a match, contest, or game in which a fight breaks out among the participants as an unplanned, spontaneous event and not as an intended part of the match, contest, or game.

So to summarize, it's illegal to beat someone up during an organized sporting event unless (1) you do it deliberately according to the official rules of those listed sports, or (2) you just do it spontaneously.

Even if I understood that, I still wouldn't be sure how to classify hockey.

IND. CODE § 35-45-18-1.

Pi has the same value in Indiana as it does everywhere else.

That'd be true no matter what the law said. But according to House Bill No. 246, which actually passed the Indiana House in 1897, the value of pi is (arguably) 3.2. Which, as you may recall, it is not.

The revaluation of pi was not immediately obvious from the text of the bill, which was based on mathematical theories devised by Dr. Edwin J. Goodwin. Dr. Goodwin—an M.D., not a Ph.D.—claimed he had "squared the circle," which refers to a very old math problem about which all we need to know right now is that it's impossible. Dr. Goodwin didn't know that, though.

He drafted a bill describing his "discovery" and convinced his representative to introduce it. House Bill No. 246 is often referred to as The Pi Bill and is described as an attempt by the legislature to set the value of pi, but it doesn't actually mention pi and in fact it doesn't look like it would have *done* anything at all. Only the title has any real "action" language:

> Bill for an act introducing a new mathematical truth and offered as a contribution to education to be used only by the State of Indiana free of cost by paying any royalties whatever on the same, provided it is accepted and adopted by the official action of the Legislature of 1897.

In other words, Goodwin was offering Indiana the right to use his "new mathematical truth" free of charge, provided the legislature "accepted and adopted" it. But a title isn't actually part of a law, and the rest of the bill just sets forth Goodwin's nonsense; it doesn't actually purport to "adopt" anything. Had it become law—and it did pass the House without dissent, before being laughed out of the Senate—it could have been argued that the favorable vote impliedly adopted its contents, but it's not like anyone would have been forced to use Goodwin's pi.

Which seems to have been 3.2, based on the claim in Section 2 that "the ratio of the diameter and circumference is as five-fourths to four[.]" One mathematician has discerned as many as seven different values for pi in Goodwin's bill, all of them wrong.

Indiana House Bill No. 246 (1897).[36]

TO SQUARE THE CIRCLE.

Claims Made That This Old Problem Has Been Solved.

The bill telling how to square a circle, introduced in the house by Mr. Record, is not intended to be a hoax. Mr. Record knows nothing of the bill with the exception that he introduced it by request of Dr. Edwin Goodwin of Posey county, who is the author of the demonstration. The latter and State Superintendent of Public Instruction Geeting believe that it is the long-sought solution of the problem, and they are seeking to have it adopted by the legislature. Dr. Goodwin, the author, is a mathematician of note. He has it copyrighted and his proposition is that if the legislature will indorse the solution he will allow the state to use the demonstration in its text-books free of charge. The author is lobbying for the bill.

"The bill . . . is not intended to be a hoax."

Indiana House Bill No. 246 (1897)

Bill for an act introducing a new mathematical truth and offered as a contribution to education to be used only by the State of Indiana free of cost by paying any royalties whatever on the same, provided it is accepted and adopted by the official action of the Legislature of 1897.

Section 1. Be it enacted by the General Assembly of the State of Indiana: It has been found that a circular area is to the square on a line equal to the quadrant of the circumference, as the area of an equilateral rectangle is to the square on one side. The diameter employed as the linear unit according to the present rule in computing the circle's area is entirely wrong, as it represents the circle's area one and one-fifth times the area of a square whose perimeter is equal to the circumference of the circle. This is because one fifth of the diameter fails to be represented four times in the circle's circumference. For example: if we multiply the perimeter of a square by one-fourth of any line one-fifth greater than one side, we can in like manner make the square's area to appear one-fifth greater than the fact, as is done by taking the diameter for the linear unit instead of the quadrant of the circle's circumference.

Section 2. It is impossible to compute the area of a circle on the diameter as the linear unit without trespassing upon the area outside of the circle to the extent of including one-fifth more area than is contained within the circle's circumference, because the square on the diameter produces the side of a square which equals nine when the arc of ninety degrees equals eight. By taking the quadrant of the circle's circumference for the linear unit, we fulfill the requirements of both quadrature and rectification of the circle's circumference. Furthermore, it has revealed the ratio of the chord and arc of ninety degrees, which is as seven to eight, and also the ratio of the diagonal and one side of a square which is as ten to seven, disclosing the fourth important fact, that the ratio of the diameter and circumference is as five-fourths to four; and because of these facts and the further fact that the rule in present use fails to work both ways mathematically, it should be discarded as wholly wanting and misleading in its practical applications.

Section 3. In further proof of the value of the author's proposed contribution to education and offered as a gift to the State of Indiana, is the fact of his solutions of the trisection of the angle, duplication of the cube and quadrature of the circle having been already accepted as contributions to science by the American Mathematical Monthly, the leading exponent of mathematical thought in this country. And be it remembered that these noted problems had been long since given up by scientific bodies as insolvable mysteries and above man's ability to comprehend.

In Kentucky, lawyers and other "public officers" must swear they have never fought a duel.

"Public officers," a term that includes not only elected officials but also people like lawyers and paramedics, must take an oath stating that:

> [S]ince the adoption of the present Constitution, I, being a citizen of this State, have not fought a duel with deadly weapons within this State nor out of it, nor have I sent or accepted a challenge to fight a duel with deadly weapons, nor have I acted as second in carrying a challenge, nor aided or assisted any person thus offending. . . .

The provision, which has been in the state constitution since 1849, was intended to deter the then-common practice of dueling (which was already illegal) by threatening the ability to hold office or practice law in the future, since if you had engaged in a duel you could not honestly swear the oath. It didn't work very well, but it's still required to this day.

In March 2010, a legislator introduced a bill to remove the dueling language, saying it was "archaic" and unseemly because it caused people to "snicker" during what was supposed to be a solemn ceremony. The bill died in committee.

Kentucky Const. § 228; S.C. CODE ANN. § 16-3-410.

In Louisiana, it's against the law to insult a boxer or wrestler during a match.

Like Indiana, Louisiana seems a little conflicted about combative sports. This statute precludes two things during a boxing or wrestling match: (1) betting, and (2) insulting the contestants:

> Open betting or quoting of odds; insulting or abusive remarks
> A. There shall be no open betting or quoting of odds in the club or arena where the exhibition or contest is being held. Whoever does so shall be ejected.
> B. There shall be no insulting or abusive remarks made by seconds, managers, or spectators and directed at the contestants. The officers of the club and the attending member of the commission shall at once eject persons who violate this or any other provision of this Chapter.

So in the context of a boxing match it's legal for you to try to beat another guy into a coma, but illegal for anyone else to insult him while you do it.

La. Rev. Stat. § 4:81.

It's illegal to jump off a bridge in Louisiana, but only if you do it to get attention.

This law appears to be aimed at the practice of "BASE jumping," an extreme sport in which people jump off tall structures with a parachute. On the other hand, it mentions only bridges *and* prohibits only jumping done to gain publicity:

> No person shall dive or jump off of any public bridge, constructed or owned by the state or any of its political subdivisions, where the object and purpose of the act is to gain publicity.
>
> Whoever violates this Section shall be fined not more than twenty-five dollars, or imprisoned for not more than thirty days, or both.

Note that it's illegal only to "dive or jump," so if you just *fall* off a bridge there seems to be no further penalty. So that's what I would advise.

La. Rev. Stat. § 14:312.

You can get 10 years of hard labor for stealing an alligator in Louisiana.

Stealing is almost always wrong, no matter what you steal, but in Louisiana they have enacted particular statutes declaring the stealing of certain wildlife to be illegal. Chief among these: the alligator.

> Theft of an alligator is the misappropriation or taking of an alligator, an alligator's skin, or a part of an alligator, whether dead or alive, belonging to another, either without the consent of the other to the misappropriation or taking, or by means of fraudulent conduct, practices, or representations. An intent to deprive the other permanently of the alligator, the alligator's skin, or a part of an alligator is essential.

It seems like this definition could be simplified to refer only to "any part of an alligator," since if somebody took a whole alligator he'd be getting all the parts, too. Also, the skin is part of an alligator. But I guess it's possible some smart guy would steal a complete alligator and then argue that my definition didn't apply, and those kinds of stupid arguments are one reason statutes are sometimes longer than they need to be.

Louisiana is serious about deterring alligator theft, too, because the law provides that if the alligator part(s) are worth more than $1,500, the alligator-stealer "shall be imprisoned, with or without hard labor," for up to *10 years*, and can also be fined up to $3,000. This doesn't seem to be out of any particular love for alligators, though, given that another statute imposes exactly the same penalties for stealing crawfish.

Stealing only *part* of a crawfish appears to be legal, but then maybe there is no market for only part of a crawfish.

La. Rev. Stat. §§ 67.13, 67.5.

You can get jail time for making noise in a Massachusetts library.

Yes, it's rude to make noise in a public library, but does it really merit jail time?

> Whoever wilfully disturbs persons assembled in a public library, or a reading room connected therewith, by making a noise or in any other manner during the time when such library or reading room is open to the public shall be punished as provided in the preceding section.

The preceding section provides for a punishment of up to a month in jail or a $50 fine for wilfully disturbing a school or other lawful assembly, so that would apply here too.

In other jurisdictions you can be jailed (and people have been) for failing to return library books, but this is the only state I'm aware of in which wilful library noisemaking is a crime.

Mass. Gen. Laws § 272-41.

In Mississippi, it's illegal to tell anyone about polygamy.

It might be okay if you're doing this to *warn* them about it rather than trying to convince them to get multi-hitched, but I'd be concerned that warning someone who didn't know that polygamy existed might be construed as "teaching" about it:

> 97-29-43. Polygamy; teaching of.
>
> If any person shall teach another the doctrines, principles, or tenets, or any of them, of polygamy; or shall endeavor so to do; or shall induce or persuade another by words or acts, or otherwise, to embrace or adopt polygamy, or to emigrate to any other state, territory, district, or country for the purpose of embracing, adopting, or practicing polygamy, or shall endeavor so to do, he shall, on conviction, be fined not less than twenty five dollars nor more than five hundred dollars, or be imprisoned in the county jail not less than one month nor more than six months, or both.

This law has never been tested in court, but it's pretty clearly unconstitutional. It's a content-based restriction on speech, and there are ways to combat polygamy, if that's what you want to do, that don't restrict speech at all (like making polygamy itself illegal).

It has been argued that making polygamy itself illegal is unconstitutional under the free-exercise clause of the First Amendment if it is practiced due to sincere religious beliefs. I think that's a pretty good argument, personally, but the Supreme Court didn't when it considered the issue in 1879:

> Polygamy has always been odious [in Europe] . . . Professor [Francis] Lieber says, polygamy leads to the patriarchal principle, and which, when applied to large communities, fetters the people in stationary despotism, while that principle cannot long exist in connection with monogamy. . . . An exceptional colony of polygamists under an exceptional leadership may sometimes exist for a time without appearing to disturb the social condition of the people who surround it; but there cannot be a doubt that, unless restricted by some form of constitution, it is within the legitimate scope of the power of every civil government to determine whether polygamy or monogamy shall be the law of social life under its dominion.

Reynolds v. United States, 98 U.S. 145, 166 (1879). The Court also compared polygamy to human sacrifice, which seems just a little extreme.

The idea that monogamy prevents despotism is also amusing.

MISS. CODE ANN. § 97-29-43.

Stallions cannot be kept in public view or within 100 yards of a church.

The law also applies to male donkeys, which are called "jacks":

SEC. 97-29-57. Stallion or jack not to be kept in public view or permitted to run at large.

A person shall not keep a stallion or jack nearer than one hundred yards to a church, or in public view in an inclosure bordering on a public highway, or nearer thereto, than one hundred yards; nor shall any person stand such animals in open view of any public place, or negligently keep such animal or suffer it to run at large. Any such offender, upon conviction, shall be fined not less than twenty-five dollars, and shall be liable for all damages done by such animals so kept or running at large.

Since the law applies only to male animals, and is in Chapter 29 of the Mississippi Code, which covers "Crimes Against Public Morals and Decency" (it's right between unlawful seduction of a female and the ban on "unnatural intercourse"), I think we can infer what embarrassment this law is intended to avoid.

Miss. Code Ann. § 97-29-57.

Wait . . . pro wrestling matches might be rigged?

Mississippi law makes it a felony to pay or solicit a bribe in exchange for trying to lose any athletic contest, with one significant exception:

> (1) Whoever gives, promises, or offers to . . . any player who participates in or expects to participate in any professional or amateur game or sport, or any person participating or expecting to participate in any other athletic contest or any coach, manager, or trainer of any team or participant or prospective participant in any such game, contest, or sport, anything of value with the intent to influence such participant to lose or try to lose or cause to be lost or to limit his or his team's margin of victory . . . shall be guilty of a felony. . . .

Subsection (2) makes it similarly illegal to solicit or accept a payment for doing this. But:

> (3) The provisions of this section shall not be deemed to include any wrestling matches, it being expressly provided hereby that wrestling matches shall be deemed to be shows or exhibitions and not athletic contests.

I'm not saying this happens in pro wrestling, of course; I'm just saying it wouldn't be against the law if it did.

MISS. CODE ANN. § 97-29-17.

In Missouri, bear wrestling and related activities are not welcome.

Actually, Missouri is one of a surprising number of states in which the practice of "bear wrestling" has been prevalent enough that the legislature has had to get involved.

Personally, I might be okay with bear wrestling under normal circumstances, since I'd be rooting for the bear and bears seem to have pretty significant natural advantages. In fact, I'd be willing to bet that no adult bear has ever lost a fair fight with a human being, *mano a mano*. But, as you might expect, people involved in this "sport" don't play fair:

> Any person who commits any of the following acts is guilty of a class A misdemeanor:
> (1) Bear wrestling;
> (2) Permitting bear wrestling to be done on any premises under his charge or control;
> (3) Promoting, conducting, or staging bear wrestling;
> (4) Advertising bear wrestling;
> (5) Collecting any admission fee for bear wrestling;
> (6) Purchasing, selling, or possessing a bear which he knows will be used for bear wrestling;
> (7) Training a bear for bear wrestling;
> (8) Subjecting a bear to surgical alteration for bear wrestling.

See, it's that last one that's the problem for me (and for the bear).

In case it isn't clear just what constitutes "bear wrestling," you might look to Louisiana, which helpfully defines the term:

> For the purposes of this Section, a "bear wrestling match" means a match or contest between one or more persons and a bear for the purpose of fighting or engaging in a physical altercation.

I guess the point is to make clear that the law applies even if Greco-Roman or other formal wrestling rules are not observed during the match.

Mo. Rev. Stat. § 578.176; La. Rev. Stat. Ann. § 102.10.

In New Hampshire, rope dancers and ventriloquists must be licensed.

Much like Delaware, in which (as noted above) even puppet shows in a private home must technically be licensed, New Hampshire has a broad prohibition on unlicensed "shows and open-air meetings":

> No showman, tumbler, rope dancer, ventriloquist or other person shall, for pay, exhibit any feats of agility, horsemanship, sleight of hand, rope dancing or feats with cards, or any animals, wax figures, puppets or other show, or promote any public competition, without a license from the selectmen of the town.
>
> No theatrical or dramatic representation shall be performed or exhibited, and no parade or procession upon any public street or way, and no open-air public meeting upon any ground abutting thereon, shall be permitted, unless a special license therefor shall first be obtained from the selectmen of the town, or from a licensing committee for cities hereinafter provided for.

These are extremely broad statutes that raise a number of questions. For example, is the first section intended to apply only to those in occupations similar to those listed ("showman, tumbler, rope dancer, [and] ventriloquist") or, as it appears to state, to any "other person" as well? If the former, what exactly is the common denominator there? I mean, we can all agree that ventriloquists should be run out of town, but what does New Hampshire have against tumbling? And was it at one time plagued by rope dancers?

If you don't want "circus folk" in town, just say so. I'd still like to see how you would define that term, but at least give it a try.

N.H. Rev. Stat. Ann. §§ 286:1-2.

New Mexico considered a law requiring certain expert witnesses to dress like wizards.

In 1995, the New Mexico Senate was debating legislation relating to expert testimony by psychologists and psychiatrists on the subject of whether a criminal defendant should be considered competent to stand trial. It would appear that at least one senator did not think such expert witnesses were generally all they were cracked up to be. I believe that because he offered an amendment that began as follows:

> When a psychologist or psychiatrist testifies during a defendant's competency hearing, the psychologist or psychiatrist shall wear a cone-shaped hat that is not less than 2 feet tall. The surface of the hat shall be imprinted with stars and lightning bolts.

The Senate adopted this measure, proving either that the senators around at that time had a good sense of humor or that they were not in the habit of reading what they voted on. (In this case I suspect the former.) Unfortunately it was removed before the bill became law (unfortunately for everybody except expert witnesses, that is), but it lives on as possibly the finest example of legislative drafting to date in the relatively short history of American law.

S. Floor Amend. 1 to S.B. 459, 42d Leg., 1st Sess. (N.M. 1995).[37]

State of New Mexico
Senate

FORTY-SECOND LEGISLATURE
FIRST SESSION, 1995

March 2, 1995

SENATE FLOOR AMENDMENT number ___/___ to SENATE BILL 459

AMENDMENT sponsored by SENATOR Duncan Scott

1. On page 2, line 11, after the period and dash, insert a new subsection designation "A.".

2. On page 3, line 1, insert a new Subsection B to read:

"B. When a psychologist or psychiatrist testifies during a defendant's competency hearing, the psychologist or psychiatrist shall wear a cone-shaped hat that is not less than two feet tall. The surface of the hat shall be imprinted with stars and lightning bolts. Additionally, a psychologist or psychiatrist shall be required to don a white beard that is not less than eighteen inches in length, and shall punctuate crucial elements of his testimony by stabbing the air with a wand. Whenever a psychologist or psychiatrist provides expert testimony regarding the defendant's competency, the bailiff shall contemporaneously dim the courtroom lights and administer two strikes to a Chinese gong.""

Senator Duncan Scott

Adopted _Margaret Larragonte_ Not Adopted _____
(Chief Clerk)   (Chief Clerk)

Date ___3/2/95___

S0459FS1

The witness shall wear a cone-shaped hat.

In New York, strangling someone is permitted only for a valid medical or dental purpose.

Under the state penal code there are three different strangulation-related offenses. The first one really seems to be attempted strangulation, but New York calls it "criminal obstruction of breathing or blood circulation":

> A person is guilty of criminal obstruction of breathing or blood circulation when, with intent to impede the normal breathing or circulation of the blood of another person, he or she:
>   a. applies pressure on the throat or neck of such person; or
>   b. blocks the nose or mouth of such person.
>   Criminal obstruction of breathing or blood circulation is a class A misdemeanor.

It becomes "strangulation in the second degree" if doing the above actually results in "stupor," unconsciousness, or "any other physical injury or impairment." It's first-degree strangulation if it causes "serious physical injury."

That part of the code then concludes by saying that for purposes of those three crimes, "it shall be an affirmative defense that the defendant performed such conduct for a valid medical or dental purpose."

There may well be such a purpose, although the only one I can think of is blocking someone's nose during mouth-to-mouth resuscitation. But if your dentist has been using this technique to put you under, you might want to shop around a bit.

N.Y. PENAL LAW §§ 121.11–.14.

Nevada funeral directors may not swear in the presence of a dead body.

This is part of the state's definition of "unprofessional conduct" on the part of a funeral director:

> [U]nprofessional conduct includes:
> 1. Misrepresentation or fraud . . .
> 2. Solicitation of dead human bodies by the licensee or his or her agents, assistants or employees, whether the solicitation occurs after death or while death is impending, but this does not prohibit general advertising.
>
>   ***
>
> 6. Gross immorality.
>
>   ***
>
> 8. Using profane, indecent or obscene language in the presence of a dead human body, or within the immediate hearing of the family or relatives of a deceased whose body has not yet been interred or otherwise disposed of.

If you deleted the second "or" from number 8, that'd be a perfectly reasonable provision. But the first clause without the second . . . I mean, it's not like anybody's gonna complain.

Ordinary citizens remain free to swear at a corpse.

NEV. REV. STAT. §§ 642.470, 642.480.

The larceny of ginseng.

"Larceny" is the crime of wrongfully acquiring the personal property of another person, or what someone who had the good sense not to go to law school would probably call "stealing." But "stealing" is a broader term than "larceny"—for example, taking something from somebody by threatening to use force is "robbery," not "larceny." Larceny is one of those crimes that was part of the common law (and still is), but most if not all states have passed specific statutes about it, and North Carolina for some reason has a fairly long list of specific things that it's illegal to larcen.

For example: This statute, first enacted in 1905, shows a special concern for one who is sufficiently evil to creep onto another man's land and get all up in his ginseng:

> § 14-79. Larceny of ginseng.
>
> If any person shall take and carry away, or shall aid in taking or carrying away, any ginseng growing upon the lands of another person, with intent to steal the same, he shall be punished as a Class H felon.

I think I like this one in particular because *The Larceny of Ginseng* sounds like it could be a Gabriel García Márquez novel. Or maybe I'm thinking of *The Unbearable Lightness of Ginseng*. One of those fancy books, anyway.

N.C. GEN. STAT. § 14-79.

In North Carolina, you will be taxed on the proceeds from rattlesnake-milking exhibitions.

Despite the risk that rattlesnake-milkers might flee the state in protest, North Carolina has imposed a tax on gross receipts:

> A rattlesnake milking exhibition for which an admission fee is charged is subject to the gross receipts tax imposed under G.S. 105-37.1.

Rattlesnake milking for charity is not taxed, however.

17 N.C. ADMIN. CODE 04B.0312 (2000).[38]

By statute, it is legal in North Carolina to ride a horse while intoxicated.

Everyone (hopefully) understands that it is against the law to operate a vehicle while intoxicated or under the influence. The exact definition of these terms varies from state to state, and one issue that has arisen many times is what qualifies as a "vehicle." For example, if you put wheels and a motor on a bar stool, could you get arrested for driving it while intoxicated? (Answer: yes.)

A more difficult question: is a horse a "vehicle" for that purpose? Not in North Carolina:

> Vehicle. – Every device in, upon, or by which any person or property is or may be transported or drawn upon a highway, excepting devices moved by human power or used exclusively upon fixed rails or tracks; provided, that for the purposes of this Chapter bicycles shall be deemed vehicles. . . .
>
> ∗∗∗
>
> Offense. – A person commits the offense of impaired driving if he drives any vehicle upon any highway, any street, or any public vehicular area within this State:
>
> (1) While under the influence of an impairing substance; or
>
> (2) After having consumed sufficient alcohol that he has, at any relevant time after the driving, an alcohol concentration of 0.08 or more. . . .; or

(3) With any amount of a Schedule I controlled substance, as listed in G.S. 90–89, or its metabolites in his blood or urine.

***

(e) Exception. – Notwithstanding the definition of "vehicle" pursuant to G.S. 20–4.01(49), for purposes of this section the word "vehicle" does not include a horse.

Most likely a rider could still be punished for recklessness, so I still wouldn't advise riding drunk.

N.C. GEN. STAT. §§ 20-4.01(49), 20-138.1.

Git yourself a hollerin' plate.

Many states issue a variety of special registration plates for motor vehicles, and North Carolina is certainly no exception. A state law lists no fewer than 227 different kinds of special plates that can be issued, many of them recognizing various honors or accomplishments like military service, or simply showing support for a particular organization.

There is also a special plate for hollerin':

> (90) Hollerin'. – Issuable to the registered owner of a motor vehicle. The plate shall bear the phrase "Hollerin'" under a representation of a person hollering on the left side of the plate. The Division may not issue the plate authorized by this subdivision unless it receives at least 300 applications for the plate.

For those unfamiliar with hollerin', it is (or was) a form of communication that was common in some rural areas prior to the advent of the telephone. One couldn't phone a neighbor to say good morning, call for help, or warn of an approaching Sasquatch, and so one would holler instead. Basically, the holler was a form of modulated yelling that one expert has compared to yodeling, but without use of the tongue. And that seems like more than enough about hollerin', except to note that the National Hollerin' Contest is held each year in Spivey's Corner, North Carolina, and that probably accounts for the hollerin' plate.

Other plates that may be available, at least if the 300-plate minimum is reached, include one reading "Don't Tread on Me" and one indicating that the owner of the vehicle is the Register of Deeds for the county, as well as plates showing support for the Maggie Valley Trout Festival, the National Wild Turkey Federation, shag dancing ("The plate may bear the phrase "I'd Rather Be Shaggin'" and a picture representing shag dancing"), sweet potatoes, and the watermelon.

N.C. Gen. Stat. § 20-79.4.[39]

But not a smoke screen.

I thought this only happened in James Bond films, but I guess not, because in North Carolina, it is specifically unlawful to install a device in your car that generates a smoke screen:

§ 20-136. Smoke screens.

(a) It shall be unlawful for any person or persons to drive, operate, equip or be in the possession of any automobile or other motor vehicle containing, or in any manner provided with, a mechanical machine or device designed, used or capable of being used for the purpose of discharging, creating or causing, in any manner, to be discharged or emitted, either from itself or from the automobile or other motor vehicle to which attached, any unusual amount of smoke, gas or other substance not necessary to the actual propulsion, care and keep of said vehicle, and the possession by any person or persons of any such device, whether the same is attached to any such motor vehicle, or detached therefrom, shall be prima facie evidence of the guilt of such person or persons of a violation of this section.

(b) Any person or persons violating the provisions of this section shall be guilty of a Class I felony.

The law was enacted in 1937 and amended in the early 1990s, so this would appear to be a continuing problem.

N.C. Gen. Stat. § 20-136.

You don't need a real-estate license to sell graves.

The same part of the North Carolina Administrative Code that contains the rattlesnake-milking tax also states that no special real-estate license is needed to sell grave plots.

> A person selling grave plots only, even though a deed is given, is exempt from real estate dealer's license [requirements].

A licensed realtor may be helpful, of course, but feel free to go with an unlicensed grave-plot seller. Hey, it's your funeral.

17 N.C. ADMIN. CODE 04B.0606 (1976).

Oklahoma's constitution guarantees religious freedom and forbids a religious practice in the same paragraph.

The first sentence of Article I, Section 2, of the Oklahoma state constitution makes a sweeping and dramatic statement in favor of religious tolerance for all.

The guy who drafted it then apparently left the room for a minute, and somebody else took the opportunity to add a sentence attacking the Mormons:

> Perfect toleration of religious sentiment shall be secured, and no inhabitant of the State shall ever be molested in person or property on account of his or her mode of religious worship; and no religious test shall be required for the exercise of civil or political rights. Polygamous or plural marriages are forever prohibited.

This constitution was adopted in 1907, just three years after the Mormon Church had renounced plural marriage (for the second time), and not long after the end of contentious hearings on whether Reed Smoot, an apostle of the church, could legally serve in the U.S. Senate. So polygamy was a big deal at the time.

It was then and remains illegal everywhere in the United States (as noted above, it is technically illegal in Mississippi even to *tell* anyone it exists), so the fact that the ban is in the Oklahoma Constitution is not especially surprising. It is just a little jarring to see it placed right after a sentence promising "perfect toleration of religious sentiment."

"Near-perfect toleration" wouldn't sound as good, but at least it'd be accurate.

Okla. Const. art. I, § 2.[40]

Oregon is the only state with an official microbe.

In 2013, Oregon became the first state in the nation to designate an official state microbe:

> Whereas Saccharomyces cerevisiae, a microorganism classified in the kingdom Fungi, has a long history of assisting in human gastronomic, cultural and scientific endeavors; and
>
> Whereas Saccharomyces cerevisiae is commonly known as brewer's yeast or baker's yeast; and
>
> Whereas dating back to ancient times, Saccharomyces cerevisiae has been used to leaven bread, converting fermentable sugars present in the dough into carbon dioxide and ethanol; and
>
> Whereas the ability to generate ethanol also makes Saccharomyces cerevisiae essential to the production of alcoholic beverages such as mead, wine, beer and distilled spirits; and
>
> Whereas Saccharomyces cerevisiae has inspired a thriving brewing culture in this state, making Oregon an internationally recognized hub of craft brewing; and
>
> Whereas Saccharomyces cerevisiae has many other important uses . . . .; now, therefore,
>
> Be It Resolved by the Legislative Assembly of the State of Oregon:
>
> That Saccharomyces cerevisiae is the official microbe of the State of Oregon.

As you may remember if you have been reading this book from the beginning as opposed to just opening it at random, perhaps without paying for it or because somebody moved your usual reading material out of the bathroom, the very first code of laws we know about refers to beer, so it is clear that beer and civilization are inextricably linked.

Wisconsin and Hawaii have both considered adopting microbes, but chickened out. Wisconsin considered Lactococcus lactis, which makes cheese, but didn't go through with it. Hawaii's candidate, Flavobacterium akiainvivens, is native to Hawaii but doesn't seem to do anything but live on the akia shrub (hence the name). Given that this one is described as forming "two- to three-millimeter diameter colonies that range from cream to off-white in color and wet to mucoid in viscosity," and is part of a genus of bacteria best known for causing various fish diseases, I think we can guess why it didn't seem to generate too much enthusiasm.

H.R. Con. Res. 12 (May 29, 2013).

No children on the fenders.

If you generally just strap your kids onto the hood when hitting the highway, you might want to avoid Oregon:

> 811.205 Carrying child on external part of vehicle; penalty.
>
> (1) A person commits the offense of carrying a child on an external part of a motor vehicle if the person carries any child upon the hood, fender, running board or other external part of any motor vehicle that is upon a highway.
>
> (2) The offense described in this section, carrying a child on an external part of a motor vehicle, is a Class B traffic violation.

We might or might not be able to infer from this language that it would be okay to do this if not driving on the highway, or that kids can be kept in the trunk. (I am not suggesting you do either thing, or frankly anything else mentioned in this book.) To me, the trunk seems like the most logical place for children, frankly, but that appears to be frowned upon.

Or. Rev. Stat. § 811.205.

Rhode Island is not actually named "Rhode Island."

It's "Rhode Island" for short, but its full name is "Rhode Island and Providence Plantations":

Constitution of the State of Rhode Island and Providence Plantations
Preamble
We, the people of the State of Rhode Island and Providence Plantations, grateful to Almighty God for the civil and religious liberty which He hath so long permitted us to enjoy, and looking to Him for a blessing upon our endeavors to secure and to transmit the same, unimpaired, to succeeding generations, do ordain and establish this Constitution of government.

Of course the state statutes sometimes just say "Rhode Island" (that probably saves a significant amount of ink each year, actually), but the official seal, official documents, and required oaths all use the full "Rhode Island and Providence Plantations." That was also the name in the Royal Charter that established the colony in 1663, and it's never been changed.

In 2010, the state legislature authorized a ballot question asking voters whether they wanted to change the name to just "Rhode Island." Supporters of the measure had argued that the "Providence Plantations" part should be dropped because the word "plantation" conjures up images of slavery and the slave trade. Maybe in the South, but (as the supporters may or may not have known) Rhode Island and

Providence Plantations was the first colony to pass antislavery legislation, which it actually did in 1652, before it was even a formal colony. That might be why the measure failed by a 56-point margin (78–22), or maybe they just like the name.

R.I. Const. art. III, § 3 (Oath of General Officers).

One shall not impersonate a corder of wood.

Several other professions are also protected from this scourge:

> Every person who shall falsely assume or pretend to be a town sealer of weights and measures, auctioneer, corder of wood, or fence-viewer, and shall act as such, shall be fined not less than twenty dollars ($20.00) nor more than one hundred dollars ($100).

A "fence-viewer" is, or was, an official who inspected fences for compliance with relevant laws. Why someone would impersonate a fence-viewer, let alone a "corder of wood," is not entirely clear, but apparently it was once a real problem.

R.I. GEN. LAWS § 11-14-2.

Keep your exploding cigars out of South Carolina.

Under state law, it's a crime to do this:

> . . . sell or possess a novelty device commonly known as a 'cigarette load' which may cause a cigarette or cigar to blow up or explode after being lit.

Information on the number of South Carolinians injured by cigarette loads over the years is difficult to come by, but I assume that number is or was at one point substantial.

S.C. CODE ANN. § 16-17-740.

It's illegal to act obnoxiously on campus.

South Carolina law makes it illegal for any person to loiter on school or college premises or "to act in an obnoxious manner thereon. . . ."

> It shall be unlawful:
>
> (1) for any person wilfully or unnecessarily (a) to interfere with or to disturb in any way or in any place the students or teachers of any school or college in this State, (b) to loiter about such school or college premises or (c) **to act in an obnoxious manner thereon;** or
>
> (2) for any person to (a) enter upon any such school or college premises or (b) loiter around the premises, except on business, without the permission of the principal or president in charge.
>
> (B) Any person violating any of the provisions of this section shall be guilty of a misdemeanor and, on conviction thereof, shall pay a fine of not more than one thousand dollars or be imprisoned in the county jail for not more than ninety days.

Emphasis added.

Presumably, this was intended to apply only to people who aren't *supposed* to be on campus, and subsection (1)(a) does refer to people who "interfere with" or disturb "students or teachers," suggesting the "people" contemplated are not part of those two groups. On the other hand, I don't see why students couldn't interfere with teachers and vice versa—my recollection is that they often do—and the other subsections don't have that language at all. So, read literally, the statute appears to make it illegal for anybody "to act in an obnoxious manner" on the premises of any school or college in South Carolina.

You might want to keep this in mind when considering where to apply.

S.C. CODE ANN. § 16-17-420.

You can't say no to a posse.

In South Carolina, if the sheriff comes by and wants you to join a posse, you join that posse or else:

> Any sheriff . . . may call out the bystanders or posse comitatus of the proper county to his assistance whenever he is resisted or has reasonable grounds to suspect and believe that such assistance will be necessary in the service or execution of process in any criminal case . . . to assist in enforcing the laws and in arresting violators or suspected violators thereof. Any person refusing to assist as one of the posse comitatus in the service or execution of such process . . . shall be liable to be indicted therefor and upon conviction shall be fined and imprisoned. . . .

If you really want to gum up the works, you could refuse to join the posse and then flee. The existing posse would either have to split into two posses, or stop to organize a completely separate posse for the job of tracking you down for the crime of refusing to join the first posse.

If everybody did this, the forced-posse system should come to a grinding halt pretty quickly.

S.C. CODE ANN. § 23-15-79.

There is no fornication in South Carolina.

"Fornication" has been illegal in South Carolina since at least 1880, presumably because the legislature wanted to have a law on the books to which no one would ever pay the slightest attention:

> Any man or woman who shall be guilty of the crime of . . . fornication shall be liable to indictment and, on conviction, shall be severally [individually] punished by a fine of not less than one hundred dollars nor more than five hundred dollars or imprisonment for not less than six months nor more than one year or by both fine and imprisonment, at the discretion of the court.

"Fornication" has a specific legal meaning under South Carolina law, and that meaning is kind of odd:

> "Fornication" is the living together and carnal intercourse with each other or habitual carnal intercourse with each other without living together of a man and woman, both being unmarried.

This law seems more concerned about living together than it does about fornication. If an unmarried couple lives together, then just one instance of "carnal intercourse" makes them both criminals. If they don't, they can intercourse all they want as long as it doesn't become a "habit."

There is no definition of "habitual."

S.C. Code Ann. §§ 16-15-60, 16-15-80.

Also no pinball or billiards.

These dangerous activities are legal for adults in South Carolina, at least, but those under 18 are forbidden from engaging in them (although billiards are allowed with parental consent):

Loitering in a billiard room.

It is unlawful for a person under eighteen years of age to loiter in a billiard or pocket billiard room or to play billiards or pocket billiards in a billiard room unless accompanied by the person's parent or guardian or with the written consent of the person's parent or guardian.

Playing pinball.

It is unlawful for a minor under the age of eighteen to play a pinball machine.

The moral dangers of billiards and pinball themselves are not immediately apparent, although I notice that both involve physics and so maybe this open and scandalous display of "science" is considered unseemly.

Assuming that the danger arises from the kind of people who are (apparently) commonly found in these locations in South Carolina, we can conclude that pinball enthusiasts are considered a much greater threat, since youth pinball is illegal even with parental consent.

S.C. CODE ANN. §§ 63-19-2420, 63-19-2430.

And no unlicensed horse-trading nomads.

It sounds a little like South Carolina has been invaded by Huns:

> It is unlawful for any nomadic individual, or bands of nomads, to encamp or to trade horses, mules, or other animals or commodities within any county of this State, without first obtaining a license from the clerk of the court. The license fee is three hundred dollars.
>
> A person who violates the provisions of this section is guilty of a misdemeanor and, upon conviction, must be fined . . . or imprisoned not more than one year, or both.

"Bands of nomads" especially makes it sound like barbarians are pouring over the border, which would be a problem because barbarians don't normally take the time to get the proper licenses.

This law, which dates back to 1918, may have been aimed at a group known as the "Irish Travellers," a nomadic group with a culture similar to that of the Roma. That group's largest settled community is in South Carolina. Whether it would be constitutional to impose this fee only on horse traders who happen to be nomadic is a question no court has yet considered.

S.C. CODE ANN. § 40-41-220.[41]

Coon-on-a-log is fine, but no hog-dogging.

Cruelty to animals is a felony in South Carolina, but there are some interesting exceptions to Title 16, Chapter 27, the "Animal Fighting and Baiting Act":

> SECTION 16-27-80. Applicability of chapter to hunting dogs and certain events.
>
> (A) This chapter does not apply to dogs used for the purpose of hunting, including, but not limited to, hunting on shooting preserves or wildlife management areas authorized pursuant to Title 50, or to dogs used in field trials, including events more commonly known as "water races", "treeing contests", "coon-on-a-log", "bear-baying", or "fox-pen-trials". Such "fox-pen-trials" must be approved by permit for field trials by the South Carolina Department of Natural Resources.
>
> (B) Except as otherwise provided in Section 16-27-60, this chapter applies to events more commonly known as "hog-dog fights", "hog-dog rodeos", or "hog-dogging" in which bets are placed, or cash, points, titles, trophies, or other awards are given based primarily on the ability of a dog to catch a hog using physical contact in the controlled environment of an enclosure.

So, to recap, coon-on-a-log is acceptable, but hog-dogging, even as part of a hog-dog rodeo, is not.

Note, however, that the ban is limited to those events that test a dog's ability to catch a hog "using physical contact." I guess this means that, if there are events in which the dog discusses existential philosophy with the hog until it agrees that life is essentially meaningless and just gives up, this law would not apply.

S.C. CODE ANN. § 16-27-80.

In South Dakota, you may use explosives to defend your crop of sunflowers.

But only from birds, and not within one-eighth of a mile of certain buildings:

> Any agricultural producer may purchase and use explosives, pyrotechnics, or fireworks for the protection of sunflower crops from depredating birds in accordance with rules promulgated pursuant to § 34-36-8. Such explosives, pyrotechnics, or fireworks may not be used within six hundred sixty feet of an occupied dwelling, church, or schoolhouse without written permission from the adjoining landowner. The governing body of any county may prohibit the use of explosives, pyrotechnics, or fireworks within its boundaries for the purposes provided in this section.

Rules were promulgated to govern the use of explosives against depredating birds, but it appears those rules were repealed in 2003. The statutory restrictions are still in effect, of course. My guess is that they decided either that counties should be able to create their own rules, or that the state was losing this war and it was time for the gloves to come off.

It is not too far from the truth to describe this as a "war." North and South Dakota, the nation's leading sunflower producers, both deploy a remarkable range of bird-defense weaponry. According to a 1997 report, these have included buzzing fields with small aircraft carrying men firing shotguns (referred to as "blackbird hazing"), two types of "propane cannons," and "pyrotechnic scare devices" called "cracker shells," "bird bangers," and "screamer sirens." Both states have also sprayed herbicide in an effort to remove large areas of cattails (where blackbirds prefer to roost), which starts to make the effort sound a little like Vietnam.

I see no evidence that the use of explosives includes carpet bombing, which would destroy the sunflowers in order to save them. Hopefully things won't escalate that far.

S.D. Codified Laws § 34-36-7.

The Tennessee constitution bars any minister, priest, atheist, or "duelist" from public office.

This has been part of Tennessee's constitution since at least 1870:

> Disqualifications.
>
> Section 1. Whereas ministers of the Gospel are by their profession, dedicated to God and the care of souls, and ought not to be diverted from the great duties of their functions; therefore, no minister of the Gospel, or priest of any denomination whatever, shall be eligible to a seat in either House of the Legislature.
>
> Section 2. No person who denies the being of God, or a future state of rewards and punishments, shall hold any office in the civil department of this state.
>
> Section 3. Any person who shall . . . fight a duel, or knowingly be the bearer of a challenge to fight a duel, or send or accept a challenge for that purpose, or be an aider or abettor in fighting a duel, shall be deprived of the right to hold any office of honor or profit in this state, and shall be punished otherwise, in such manner as the Legislature may prescribe.

It's a violation of the First Amendment to bar someone from office because of his or her religious beliefs, but duelists are pretty much out of luck.

Tenn. Const. art. IX, §§ 1–3 (2012) (adopted 1870).

Don't bring your skunks into Tennessee.

I was not aware there was a thriving interstate skunk trade, but apparently there is or was at one point:

> 70-4-208. Unlawful importation of skunks -- Penalty.
>
> (a) It is unlawful for any person to import, possess, or cause to be imported into this state any type of live skunk, or to sell, barter, exchange or otherwise transfer any live skunk, except that the prohibitions of this section shall not apply to bona fide zoological parks and research institutions.
>
> (b) A violation of this section is a Class C misdemeanor.

I guess it is not illegal to import or possess a *dead* skunk. It seems highly unlikely anyone would do that, but then I can't think of a reason to bring in live ones, either.

Tenn. Code Ann. § 70-4-208.

Texas once had a five-"device" limit.

It is technically illegal in Texas to "promote" or "possess with intent to promote" any "obscene device," which is defined as one "designed or marketed as useful primarily for the stimulation of human genital organs." It would be unconstitutional to ban such devices, so Texas grudgingly settled for criminalizing their "promotion."

That turned out to be unconstitutional, too, but the law is still on the books.

Interestingly, "possession with intent to promote" is also a crime. How might one determine whether a possessor of such an item had that specific intent or . . . well, some other intent? Texas appears to have looked to the example of drug laws, which presume an "intent to distribute" if a suspect possesses more than a defined quantity. Here:

> [a] person who possesses six or more obscene devices or identical or similar obscene articles is presumed to possess them with intent to promote the same.

Why the legal limit should be *five* remains a mystery.

TEX. PENAL CODE §§ 43.21(a)(7), 43.23(c), 43.23(f) & 43.23(g).[42]

The five-device limit did not apply to legislators.

Interestingly, the Texas obscene-device-promotion ban just previously mentioned did not apply if:

> a person who possesses or promotes material or a device proscribed by this section does so for a bona fide medical, psychiatric, judicial, legislative, or law enforcement purpose.

What "bona-fide legislative purpose" did the legislators who passed this have in mind? That is a great question. Please ask the next one you meet.

TEX. PENAL CODE § 43.23(g).

The Texas legislature once passed a resolution honoring Albert DeSalvo.

In 1971, the Texas House of Representatives passed the following resolution honoring a remarkable American:

> WHEREAS, The Honorable Albert De Salvo has unselfishly served his country, his state, and his community . . . ; and
>
> WHEREAS, Widely esteemed for his knowledge and unique skill, his outstanding service to the public has won him recognition as a model of active citizenship, a champion of worthwhile causes, and an acknowledged leader in his singular field; and
>
> WHEREAS, He has been officially recognized . . . for his noted activities and unconventional techniques involving population control and applied psychology; and
>
> WHEREAS, Above all, this compassionate gentleman's dedication and devotion to his work has enabled the weak and lonely, throughout the nations, to achieve and maintain a new degree of concern for their future; now therefore, be it
>
> RESOLVED, That the House of Representatives of the 62nd Legislature of the State of Texas commend Albert De Salvo on his outstanding career of public service. . . .

This is funny because Albert DeSalvo was better known as the "Boston Strangler."

BOSTON STRANGLER   62nd Leg. 1971   C.1.

Memo File

BY *Moore of*
Mc Lennon   H.S.R. NO._____

RESOLUTION

WHEREAS, The Honorable Albert De Salvo has unselfishly served his country, his state, and his community; and

WHEREAS, His sincerity diligence, and cooperation has earned him the warm admiration and affection of his fellow practictioners; and

WHEREAS, Widely esteemed for his knowledge and unique skill, his outstanding service to the public has won him recognition as a model of active citizenship, a champion of worthwhile causes, and an acknowledged leader in his singular field; and

WHEREAS, He has been officially recognized by the State of Massachusetts for his noted activities and unconventional techniques involving population control and applied psychology; and

WHEREAS, Albert De Salvo's singular achievements have brought about significant contributions to the fields of medicine and mental health; and

WHEREAS, Above all, this compassionate gentleman's dedication and devotion to his work has enabled the weak and lonely, throughout our nation, to achieve and maintain a new degree of concern for their future; now therefore, be it

RESOLVED, That the House of Representatives of the 62nd Legislature of the State of Texas commend Albert De Salvo on his outstanding career of public service; and be it further

RESOLVED, That a copy of this Resolution, under the seal of the House of Representatives, be prepared for Albert De Salvo as a token of the continued good wishes of the Texas House of Representatives.

He seemed like such a nice young man.

DeSalvo confessed in 1967 to 13 murders, though he later recanted and, at the time, there was no other hard evidence linking him to those crimes. He was convicted of other charges and given a life sentence the same year, all of which was widely reported. So there were good reasons in 1971 to expect people to know who he was. Either Texas legislators didn't, or—and this may have been the point—legislators don't always read before voting.

You'd think they would make an exception for measures introduced on April Fool's Day, but not this time.

H.S.R. No. [Unknown], 62d Leg., Reg. Sess. (Tex. 1971).[43]

Virginia observes "Motherhood and Apple Pie Day."

January 26 is "Motherhood and Apple Pie Day" in the state of Virginia:

> The twenty-sixth day of January of each year shall be recognized and celebrated as Motherhood and Apple Pie Day throughout the Commonwealth. Upon this date, all citizens of the Commonwealth are urged to reflect upon the need to continue efforts to reduce the state's infant mortality rate to preserve our heritage and to ensure the health and well-being of future generations.

I haven't been able to find records of the vote on this legislation, but it seems highly unlikely that anyone voted against it.

VA. CODE ANN. § 2.2-3303.

It's illegal in Virginia
for shoe stores to X-ray
a customer's feet.

A number of states, including Virginia, have laws against using X-ray equipment on someone's feet in order to (purportedly) create custom footwear:

> It shall be unlawful for any person to use any X ray, fluoroscope, or other equipment or apparatus employing roentgen rays, in the fitting of shoes or other footwear. This section shall not apply to any licensed physician or surgeon in the practice of his profession. Any person violating the provisions of this section shall be guilty of a Class 3 misdemeanor.

Starting in the 1920s, when portable X-ray technology was still relatively new, it became a fairly common practice for shoe stores to deploy this technology and claim that it would help fit shoes properly. As Jacob Lowe's patent application in 1919 put it:

> One of the most difficult things in regard to the purchasing of ready-made boots and shoes is the task of obtaining a fit. The new shoes may feel alright for the first few minutes, but after wearing them for a few blocks a painful pressure assures the owner that he has again made a failure in his desire to get neat looking but comfortable shoes. . . . To this end I have so disposed x-ray apparatus as to enable the positions of the bones of

the foot within the new shoe to be clearly seen. . . , whereby any cramping or compression of the toes is instantly made apparent.

Eventually, state legislatures decided this was more of a publicity stunt than a leap forward in shoe science, and quite a few of them banned the practice, hoping to protect consumers from bogus claims.

As you can see, though, they did concede that X-rays might be useful if the person interpreting the X-ray was a medically trained professional rather than a shoe salesman.

VA. CODE ANN. § 18.2-321.

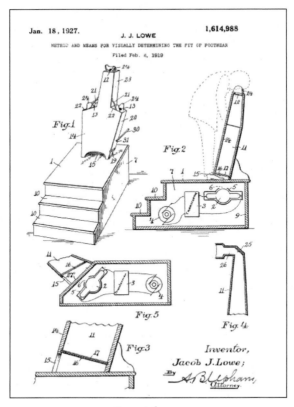

Step right up.

Washington has an official state mammoth.

More accurately, the mammoth (Mammuthus columbi) is the "official state fossil."

Mammoths did once roam around what is now Washington:

> The legislature recognizes that the large, hairy prehistoric elephants of the extinct genus Mammuthus roamed the North American continent, including the Pacific Northwest, during the Pleistocene epoch (ice ages).

Sadly, the mammoths became extinct once their natural habitat had been entirely replaced by Starbucks locations.

WASH. REV. CODE ch. 1.20.042.

Washington's official state folk song celebrates the river that ties its snowcapped mountains to the ocean so blue.

It appears there has been at least one frustrated poet in the Washington Legislature:

> The legislature recognizes that winter recreational activities are part of the folk tradition of the state. . . . Winter recreational activities serve to turn the darkness of a northwest winter into the dawn of renewed vitality. As the winter snows dissolve into the torrents of spring, the Columbia river is nourished. The Columbia river is the pride of the northwest and the unifying geographic element of the state. In order to celebrate the river which ties the winter recreation playground of snowcapped mountains and the Yakima, Snake, and the Klickitat rivers to the ocean so blue, the legislature declares that the official state folk song is "Roll On Columbia, Roll On," composed by Woody Guthrie.

Ironically, perhaps, Guthrie wrote this song and the rest of the "Columbia River Ballads" after being commissioned to do so by the federal government, which was trying to drum up support for massive hydroelectric projects on the river.

WASH. REV. CODE § 1.20.073.

It's illegal to shoot fish in Wyoming.

In a barrel or otherwise:

> No person shall take, wound or destroy any fish of Wyoming with a firearm of any kind or nature.

This is despite the fact that even wounding a fish would probably be a fairly challenging shot and so could be considered sporting. It's hard to say how common it is for people to try to fish with firearms, but Wyoming is not the only state to ban this by any means.

It would appear, though, that the law protects only the "fish of Wyoming," so fish from other states may want to think twice before migrating there.

Wyo. Stat. Ann. § 23-3-201(d).

The official state code of Wyoming is "the code of the West," also known as "cowboy ethics."

According to a Wyoming statute, the official state code is "the code of the West," derived from the book *Cowboy Ethics* by James P. Owen. The law summarizes this code as follows:

> Live each day with courage;
> Take pride in your work;
> Always finish what you start;
> Do what has to be done;
> Be tough, but fair;
> When you make a promise, keep it;
> Ride for the brand;
> Talk less, say more;
> Remember that some things are not for sale; and
> Know where to draw the line.

These are mostly self-explanatory, but to learn what "ride for the brand" means, you may need to read the book, as the law does not explain.

Just FYI, Wyoming also has an *official* official state code, and — assuming there is a conflict — that's the one you should follow.

Wyo. Stat. Ann. 8-3-123.

PART FIVE

The Laws of the Cities of the States of the United States

The longest known legal definition of "buttocks."

St. Johns County, Florida, has a spectacular 316-word example, intended to define what must be covered by bathers or dancers. Behold:

> <u>Buttocks</u>: The area at the rear of the human body (sometimes referred to as the glutaeus maximus) which lies between two imaginary straight lines running parallel to the ground when a person is standing, the first or top such line being 1/2 inch below the top of the vertical cleavage of the nates (i.e., the prominence formed by the muscles running from the back of the hip to the back of the leg) and the second or bottom such line being 1/2 inch above the lowest point of the curvature of the fleshly protuberance (sometimes referred to as the gluteal fold), and between two imaginary straight lines, one on each side of the body (the "outside lines"), which outside lines are perpendicular to the ground and to the horizontal lines described above and which perpendicular outside lines pass through the outermost point(s) at which each nate meets the outer side of each leg. Notwithstanding the above, Buttocks shall not include the leg, the hamstring muscle below the gluteal fold, the tensor fasciae latae muscle or any of the above described portion of the human body that is between either (i) the left inside perpendicular line and the left outside perpendicular line or (ii) the right inside perpendicular line and the right outside perpendicular line. For the purpose of the previous sentence the left inside perpendicular line shall be an imaginary straight line on the left side of the anus (i) that is perpendicular to the ground and

to the horizontal lines described above and (ii) that is 1/3 of the distance from the anus to the left outside line, and the right inside perpendicular line shall be an imaginary straight line on the right side of the anus (i) that is perpendicular to the ground and to the horizontal lines described above and (ii) that is 1/3 of the distance from the anus to the right outside line.

A final sentence helpfully summarizes this as "1/3 of the buttocks centered over the cleavage for the length of the cleavage."

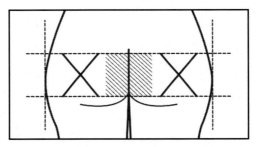

Shaded portion represents the "buttocks" as defined by law; note substantial difference between legal and commonly understood meaning.

Surprisingly—if you can still be surprised at this point in the book—this definition is now fairly common. That's because in the 1990s the St. Johns ordinance was challenged on First Amendment grounds (dancing can be considered "expression," you see), and ultimately was upheld. So local governments that wanted to limit buttock displays could adopt this language with some confidence that the law would be found constitutional if challenged.

In an excellent example of why complicated laws are a bad idea, however, at least one town appears to have copied it incorrectly. Until and unless it's fixed, that town's version arguably requires all of the left buttock to be covered but none of the right, which is probably not what they had in mind.

St. Johns County, Fla. Ord. 1992-12.[44]

An Arkansas city council banned all unapproved meetings or organizations.

In 2011, the city council of Gould, Arkansas, passed this:

> [Neither] the Mayor nor City Council members shall attend or participate in any meetings with any organization in any location without City Council approval by [a two-thirds vote].
>
> The Gould Citizens Advisory Council . . . is hereby banned from doing business in the City of Gould. . . . [T]he said Council is, in effect, causing confusion and discourse among the citizens of Gould and as a result is contributing to the friction not only between the Mayor and Council but also among the citizens. . . . Also no new organizations shall be allowed to exist in the City of Gould without approval from a majority of the City Council.

If it strikes you as odd for a law to ban meetings and organizations without prior government approval, that's probably because—unlike the council majority—you know that the First Amendment protects freedom of association. Gould's city attorney told the council the ordinance was unconstitutional, and it responded by trying to fire him.

After talking to council members and the mayor, local reporters contacted John DiPippa, dean of the University of Arkansas at Little Rock's law school, to get his opinion. He agreed that the ordinance was an unconstitutional "embarrassment," noting that the ban on "organizations" was so broad it would extend to church groups, garden clubs, and pretty much any other association between two or more people inside city limits.

"Technically," he told the reporters, "when [the council members] met with you, they violated their own ordinance."

GOULD, ARK., CITY ORDINANCE no. 062011.4, 062011.5.[45]

In San Francisco, a necromancer needs to have an official fortunetelling permit.

You might not think you'd need a permit to do something that is total bullshit, but think again:

> **Fortunetelling shall mean the telling of fortunes**, forecasting of futures, or reading the past, by means of any occult, psychic power, faculty, force, clairvoyance, cartomancy, psychometry, phrenology, spirits, tea leaves, tarot cards, scrying, coins, sticks, dice, sand, coffee grounds, crystal gazing or other such reading, or through mediumship, seership, prophecy, augury, astrology, palmistry, **necromancy**, mindreading, telepathy or other craft, art, science, talisman, charm, potion, magnetism, magnetized article or substance, [or] effecting spells, charms, or incantations, or placing, or removing curses . . . in order, for example, to get or recover property, stop bad luck, give good luck, put bad luck on a person or animal, stop or injure the business or health of a person or shorten a person's life, obtain success in business, enterprise, speculation and games of chance, win the affection of a person, . . . or other such similar activity.

Most of you probably knew that fortune-telling includes "the telling of fortunes," but may have been unsure about necromancy. Now you know.

S.F., CAL., MUN. CODE art. 17.1, § 1302(a)–(c) (2003) (emphasis added).

245

You can't be naked in public, unless you're in a parade.

One of the many things of which San Francisco has long been tolerant is public nudity. That has been especially true in the city's famous Castro District and at a variety of annual events ranging from the Gay Pride Parade to the "Bay to Breakers" seven-mile road race. Over the past few years, though, that has begun to change.

The practice seems to have been sufficiently popular in the Castro that in 2011, the district's own representative decided it had gotten a little out of hand, and introduced legislation to restrict it. As a result, under Police Code section 1071.1(b), customers in public restaurants are now actually required to wear pants:

> Except as provided herein, every person is guilty of an infraction who, (1) while present as a customer in the public eating and drinking areas of an establishment whose primary purpose is to serve food, exposes his or her genitals, buttocks, or anal region . . .

Shorts would also be acceptable. They just want to establish coverage, not a dress code.

Beyond that—and to some further outcry from the affected community—the law also made it illegal for the first time to sit on public benches, steps, or similar seating areas without "clothing or other separate material" between the sitter and the thing sat upon. Note that clothing *per se* appeared to be optional.

In 2013, things became even more dire for the pro-nude, when an amendment to a different section of the code went so far as to require *pants in any public place.* The new section specifically says it does not supersede existing nudity laws (this has to do with strip clubs, I believe), *except* for the aforementioned section on outdoor sitting. Therefore, the new law plainly squelches the idea that one could sit pants-free as long as a separate barrier had been deployed.

There is one very notable exception to the bottomless-nudity ban: parades.

"Parades, fairs, and festivals" are exempt so long as the city has granted the necessary permits. This gives you some idea of the nature of some of San Francisco's parades, fairs, and festivals, as well as the political clout of those who enjoy them.

I have mixed feelings on this one. This is not an activity I personally would engage in or even enjoy being within sight of, but I think it's a good thing overall to live in a generally tolerant society. On the other hand, I have a vested interest in being able to write things like, "In San Francisco you now can't be naked in public unless you are in a parade." So on the whole, I'd have to say I'm comfortable with the law as it now stands.

S.F., CAL., POLICE CODE §§ 154, 1071.1(b).[46]

Snowball fights are illegal in Aspen, Colorado.

Seriously. No exceptions.

> It shall be unlawful for any person to throw any stone, snowball or other missile, or discharge any bow, blowgun, slingshot, gun, catapult, or other device, upon or at any vehicle, building, or other public or private property, or upon or at any person, or in any public way or place which is public in nature.

Even worse, they won't let you use your catapult. Granted, using a catapult to win a snowball fight could be considered cheating anyway.

ASPEN, COLO., MUN. CODE § 15.04.210.

It's illegal in Columbus, Georgia, to wear a tall hat in a theater.

And if you are the proprietor, you cannot allow anyone to wear such a head covering:

> It shall be unlawful for any person to wear a hat or any other covering of the head which obstructs the view of other persons, in any theater, opera house, motion picture theater or any other building where an entertainment is given and an admission charged, during any performance at such theater, opera house, motion picture theater or any other building where an entertainment is given and an admission charged.
>
> It shall be unlawful for any proprietor, manager, or any other person in charge of any theater, opera house, motion picture theater, or any other building where an entertainment is given and an admission is charged to permit any person to wear a hat, or any other covering of the head which obstructs the view of other persons in any theater, opera house, motion picture theater or any other building where an entertainment is given and an admission charged.

This certainly makes sense but you'd like to think a law wouldn't be required here.

It may have been more necessary when Columbus established (or last codified) its municipal code, which seems to have been in 1914, judging from the date of most of these provisions. Hats were taller then, of course.

The code also still requires steamboat captains to deliver any offender to the shore authorities, and prohibits using a fictitious name at a hotel, swearing on the telephone, or imitating a fire whistle. Public dances "must be conducted in a manner free from behavior calculated to offend a sense of common decency or morality," meaning no prostitutes, no persons under the influence of liquor, and for dances attended by minors there must be at least four chaperones, two of whom must be off-duty policemen.

It's probably more fun in Columbus these days, or at least I hope it is.

COLUMBUS, GA., MUN. CODE §§ 4-4, 14-18, 14-20, 14-49, 14-60.

No dogs at Corn Fest.

You can't even carry one down the street:

18.11 DOGS PROHIBITED AT CORN FEST.

It shall be unlawful for any person to walk or carry a dog upon any public way within the Central Business District from Friday at 8:00 a.m. through Sunday at 6:00 p.m. during the annual DeKalb Corn Fest.

Persons violating this section shall be fined not less than Fifty Dollars ($50.00) nor more than One Hundred Dollars ($100.00) for each offense.

Research has not revealed what dogs did to be so completely excluded from Corn Fest, although I think we can hazard a guess.

DeKalb, Ill., Mun. Code § 18.11.

251

Chico, California, does not allow its residents to have nuclear weapons.

Having found that the possibility of nuclear war is a "clear and present danger" to the citizens of the Chico community, the city council decided to declare the city a "nuclear free zone":

> Prohibition on the production, testing, maintenance and storage of nuclear weapons and nuclear weapons delivery systems.
>
> No person shall produce, test, maintain, or store within the city a nuclear weapon, component of a nuclear weapon, nuclear weapon delivery system, or component of a nuclear weapon delivery system.

Unfortunately, they forgot to make it illegal to actually set one *off* in Chico (except for testing purposes), so assuming you could get it inside the city limits without getting a ticket for possession of a nuclear weapon, you can feel free to light it up.

On the other hand, that might violate city noise regulations, which prohibit any noise level greater than 70 decibels (60 at night).

CHICO, CAL., MUN. CODE § 9.60.

The juggler's defense.

Boulder, Colorado, has very specific rules about what visitors to the Pearl Street mall may cast, throw, or propel:

> Section 5-6-9 (Projectiles on Mall):
> (a) No person shall cast, throw, or propel any projectile on the mall. This prohibition includes, without limitation, throwing balls, boomerangs, bottles, darts, frisbees and other like devices, model airplanes, rocks, snowballs, and sticks.
> (b) This section does not apply to a juggler if the juggler does not cast, throw, or propel a knife, including, without limitation, a knife with a blade three and one-half inches in length or less, or [a] burning projectile . . . .

As you can see, section (b) exempts jugglers from the projectile prohibition, thus allowing them to juggle so long as they do not juggle knives of any size or any item that is on fire. Given the wide range of other dangerous items that could still be legally juggled (grenades come to mind), I'm not sure why the ordinance is written this way. Why not something like "This section does not apply to a juggler so long as what the juggler is juggling could not kill or injure anyone except under the most ridiculous and probably comical circumstances"?

Hey, it's better than what they have now.

In 2006, a judge had to interpret this ordinance after a high-school student was ticketed for playing "Hacky Sack" (also, horribly, known as "footbagging"). The footbagger was charged with propelling a projectile, but argued that he had in fact been "juggling," invoking the limited juggler's defense provided by Section 5-6-9(b). This failed, most likely because the common meaning of "juggle" seems to require more than one object and/or participant, and if so then solo unijugglers will always be out of luck. The judge did reduce the fine substantially, however.

BOULDER, COLO., ORD. § 5-6-9.

Fort Wayne needs to revise its locomotive-bell-ringing rules.

I feel a little sorry for locomotive engineers and conductors who have to travel through Fort Wayne, Indiana, because for the last 20 years or so they must have been completely baffled by what if anything to do with the bell.

First, there's this:

> It shall be the duty of every engineer, conductor or other person engaged in running any locomotive, to ring the bell attached to such locomotive whenever the locomotive shall be moving in or through the city.

Okay, well, that's clear enough. Then there's this:

> It shall be unlawful for any person running or controlling any locomotive to sound the whistle thereof or allow the whistle to be sounded within the corporate limits of the city, unless to prevent accidents that cannot otherwise be arrested.

So the bell is for general warning purposes but the whistle is reserved for emergencies. All right. But then this:

> It shall be unlawful, within the city, for any engineer, conductor or person in charge of any engine or train of cars, to blow the whistle or ring the bell of any such engine or train . . . immediately prior to or while in the process of crossing over [five listed

intersections]. The engineer, conductor or person in charge of any engine or train of cars, shall follow all rules and regulations set down by OSHA and state statute regarding the blowing of whistles and the ringing of bells while traveling in the city limits and crossing over all other city streets except those specifically mentioned in this section.

So: It's unlawful not to ring the bell constantly in town but also unlawful to ring the bell in one part of town. And it's unlawful not to follow federal and state bell-ringing laws (something that would be unlawful anyway) except when Fort Wayne says otherwise (something it can't legally do). Got it.

FORT WAYNE, IND., MUN. CODE §§ 98.21–.23.

The city code of Joliet, Illinois, tells you how to pronounce "Joliet."

There's no penalty for getting it wrong, but mispronunciation is "discouraged":

> The only official, correct and proper pronunciation and spelling of the name of this city shall be Jo-li-et; the accent on the first syllable, with the "o" in the first syllable pronounced in its long sound, as in the words "so," "no" and "foe" and any other pronunciations to be discouraged as interfering with the desired uniformity in respect to the proper pronunciation of the name of this city.

So now you know.

JOLIET, ILL., MUN. CODE § 2-8.

Flirting remains illegal in Haddon Township, New Jersey.

The title of the ordinance is "Offending or annoying persons in public places," but it is indeed broad enough to criminalize flirting:

> Whoever accosts or approaches any person of the opposite sex unknown to such person and by word, sign or gesture attempts to speak to or to become acquainted with such person against his will, on a public street or other public place in the Township, except in the transaction of legitimate business, or whoever attempts to entice or procure a person of the opposite sex to commit an unlawful act, or whoever accosts or approaches any person and by word, sign or gesture suggests or invites the doing of any indecent or unnatural act, shall, upon conviction thereof, be punished as provided in this chapter.

An earlier ordinance in the same section makes it illegal to "willfully obstruct, molest, hinder, annoy, frighten, threaten, insult or interfere with" anyone in a public place, so this one must mean something other than just bothering people; and it certainly seems to be concerned with sex or at least potential sex, or maybe dancing.

Three kinds of situations are covered: (1) someone tries to "become acquainted with" a stranger of the opposite sex against that person's will—though of course you wouldn't know whether they objected until after you spoke to them—unless it's for "legitimate business," whatever that might be; (2) someone tries to "entice" one of the opposite sex to "commit an unlawful act," presumably one to which the person's sex is relevant; and (3) someone approaches a stranger—this time of either sex—and "suggests or invites the doing of any indecent or unnatural act."

We could parse this out further, but unless it is construed so narrowly that it would apply only to actual harassment, it's pretty clearly unconstitutional. So it seems fairly safe to flirt in Haddon Township, unless you're *really* bad at it.

HADDON TOWNSHIP, N.J., MUN. CODE §§ 1-15, 175-12.

You can't throw "marine life" during a Mardi Gras parade.

Most probably know that it's customary to throw beads during Mardi Gras parades. But the custom also seems to have extended to more unusual items:

(a) No Mardi Gras parade participant, while participating in a parade on the parade route, in a parade staging area or in a parade disbanding area, shall possess or have in his custody or control any of the following:

(1) Any life-threatening objects or safety-threatening objects, including, but not limited to "bomb bags";

(2) Any noxious substance or any liquid intended to be poured, tossed, handed out or otherwise distributed;

(3) Any throw containing sharp points, including but not limited to plastic spears or plastic, paper or silk flowers with wire stems;

(4) Any insects, marine life, rodents, fowl or other animals, dead or alive.

I wouldn't be too concerned about the occasional insect, frankly, but I am glad it's illegal to fling "marine life." A flying manatee could do some real damage. (Louisiana does not specifically criminalize manatee harassment, but remember that the manatee is protected by federal law as well.)

The throwing of cardboard boxes, "sexually-oriented devices," and certain kinds of doubloons is also prohibited.

NEW ORLEANS, LA., CODE § 34-28.

In New Orleans, one may not set forth one's power to turn bitterest enemies into staunchest friends.

This is one of the many anti-fortune-telling ordinances in cities and towns across the United States, but as written it seems to go well beyond that particular business. In particular, the "set forth his power" portion does not seem connected to any of the usual psychic disciplines:

> **It shall be unlawful for any person** to advertise for or engage in, for a monied consideration, the business of (chronology, phrenology, astrology, palmistry), telling or pretending to tell fortunes, either with cards, hands, water, letters or other devices or methods, or to hold out inducements, either through the press or otherwise, or **to set forth his power to** settle lovers' quarrels, to bring together the separated, to locate buried or hidden treasures, jewels, wills, bonds or other valuables, to remove evil influences, to give luck, to effect marriages, to heal sickness, to reveal secrets, **to foretell the results of lawsuits**, business transactions, investments of whatsoever nature, wills, deeds and/or mortgages, to locate lost or absent friends or relatives, to reveal, remove and avoid domestic troubles **or to bring together the bitterest enemies converting them into staunchest friends.** But nothing herein contained shall apply to any branch of medical science, or to any religious worship.

I guess there could be a psychic or magic power that is used to "bring together the bitterest enemies converting them into staunchest friends," maybe the same branch that makes love potions, but the language used is kind of odd.

The part making it illegal "to foretell the results of lawsuits" makes me wonder whether lawyers are covered by this thing, especially since, unlike medical science and religion, there is no specific exclusion for the law.

NEW ORLEANS, LA., CODE § 54-312 (Code 1956, § 42-91) (emphasis added).

New Orleans also defines a "Peeping Tom" as "one who peeps."

This could probably have been done more simply:

Sec. 54-279. - Peeping Tom.

(a) It shall be unlawful for any person to perform such acts as will make him a peeping Tom on or about the premises of another, or go upon the premises of another for the purpose of becoming a peeping Tom.

(b) For the purpose of this section, peeping Tom means one who peeps through windows or doors, or other like places, situated on or about the premises of another for the purpose of spying upon or invading the privacy of persons spied upon without the consent of the persons spied upon.

If you think about it for a while, "peeping Tom" is harder to define than it seems at first, although on the other hand "one who peeps" might cover it. The reference to "peeping Tom" is not really necessary, since you could just make the act itself illegal rather than make it illegal to "perform such acts as will make [one] a peeping Tom," and then try to describe what it is that peeping Toms do, i.e., peep.

NEW ORLEANS, LA., CODE § 54-279 (Code 1956, § 42-90).

It's unlawful in Oklahoma City to tattoo a fish.

Or to smuggle in fish that have been tattooed elsewhere:

(a) It shall be unlawful for any person to dye or artificially color or cause to be dyed or artificially colored any mammal, bird, reptile, or amphibian, including wild and domesticated species or to bring or transport any dyed or artificially colored mammal, bird, reptile, or amphibian, including wild and domesticated species into the City.

(b) It shall be unlawful for any person to tattoo any fish or to cause any fish to be tattooed or to bring or transport any tattooed fish into the City.

(c) It shall be unlawful for any person to artificially color any fish or cause any fish to be artificially colored or to bring or transport any artificially colored fish into the City when the artificial coloring is a result of the injection of dyes into the fish through the use of needles or other invasive techniques.

Note that it's not illegal to change the color of a fish as long as it's not done "invasively," such as with tattoo needles. How did this come about?

Responding to the view that any artificial coloring of animals is inhumane, in 2006 the city council banned the practice entirely. In 2007, a pet-store customer reported spotting a fish with "I love you" tattooed on its scales, and the city swung into action. According to

the owner of the pet-supply company that sold the fish, the city con-
fiscated $1,700 worth of tattooed fish and euthanized them, which if
true would mean it made its point about animal rights by murdering a
bunch of fish.

The owner protested not only the heavy-handed tactics of the "fish
police," as he called them, but also the total ban, which he said threat-
ened his business and the livelihoods of the 115 people who worked
there. The amended ordinance above was a compromise that allows
them to go on coloring fish as long as they don't use "invasive techniques." The incident therefore did improve the living conditions of
Oklahoma City fish to some extent, except for the dead ones.

OKLA. CITY, OKLA., MUN. CODE § 8-117 (2010).

In Portland, Oregon, all skeleton-scraping must take place indoors.

The obvious question here is what in God's name has been going on in Portland, but I'm not sure I want to know the answer:

> 8.36.160 Cleaning Skeletons.
>
> It is unlawful to scrape or clean the skeleton of any dead body in any burial ground within the City, except in a suitable building erected thereon. It is unlawful to deposit any scrapings or dead matter from any skeleton or dead body in any burial ground in said City in such manner as to expose the scrapings or dead matter to public view.

Note that the ordinance bans skeleton-scraping only "in any burial ground" within city limits, but I wouldn't count on them looking the other way if you decided to scrape your skeleton at the mall or something like that. At least stay clear of the food court, would you please?

PORTLAND, ORE., CODE ch. 8.36.160.

Cross-dressing without a permit is illegal in Walnut City, California.

Honestly, I assumed this one wasn't real when I read about it, but it is in fact on the books in Walnut City, a municipality within Los Angeles County:

> 17-31 Male dressing as female.
> No man or boy shall dress as a girl or woman without a permit from the sheriff, except for the purpose of amusement, show or drama.

Obviously this is illegal only for men, which is at least the second reason it is almost certainly unconstitutional.

The same code prohibits begging by any "person of the class commonly known as 'tramps'" (17-8), picking flowers in a public place without permission (17-25), or, in parks, engaging in any voluntary parachute jumps (luckily, it looks like *involuntary* ones are still okay) (17-25.1(b)(9)), throwing spears ((b)(10)), disturbing trees ((b)(13)), firing torpedoes ((b)(24)), or landing any "aeroplane, airship, flying machine, dirigible, balloon, parachute or other instrumentality, machine or apparatus for aviation" ((b)(23)).

The city of Fort Dodge, Iowa, also has an ordinance making it unlawful for any person to appear in a public place "in a dress not belonging to his or her own sex," but at least that one doesn't discriminate.

WALNUT CITY, CAL., MUN. CODE § 17-31; FORT DODGE, IOWA, MUN. CODE § 9.20.110.

The emergency
Sasquatch ordinance.

In 1969, the board of commissioners for Skamania County, Washington, a heavily forested county in the Cascade Mountains, adopted an ordinance stating that the "premeditated, wilful and wanton slaying" of a Sasquatch would thenceforth be considered a felony:

> WHEREAS, there is evidence to indicate the possible existence in Skamania County of a nocturnal primate mammal variously described as an ape-like creature or a sub-species of Homo Sapian [sic], and
>
> WHEREAS, this creature is generally and commonly known as a "Sasquatch," "Yeti," "Bigfoot," or "Giant Hairy Ape," and
>
> WHEREAS, publicity attendant upon such real or imagined sightings has resulted in an influx of scientific investigators as well as casual hunters, many armed with lethal weapons, and
>
> WHEREAS, the absence of specific laws covering the taking of specimens encourages laxity in the use of firearms ... and poses a clear and present threat to [citizens] as well as to the creatures themselves,
>
> THEREFORE BE IT RESOLVED that any premeditated, wilful and wanton slaying of any such creature shall be deemed a felony punishable by a fine not to exceed Ten Thousand Dollars ($10,000.00) and/or imprisonment in the county jail for a period not to exceed Five (5) years.
>
> BE IT FURTHER RESOLVED that the situation existing constitutes an emergency and as such this ordinance is effective immediately.

ORDINANCE NO. 69-01

BE IT HEREBY ORDAINED BY THE BOARD OF COUNTY COMMISSIONERS OF SKAMANIA COUNTY:

WHEREAS, there is evidence to indicate the possible existence in Skamania County of a nocturnal primate mammal variously described as an ape-like creature or a sub-species of Homo Sapian; and

WHEREAS, both legend and purported recent sightings and spoor support this possibility, and

WHEREAS, this creature is generally and commonly known as a "Sasquatch", "Yeti", "Bigfoot", or "Giant Hairy Ape", and

WHEREAS, publicity attendant upon such real or imagined sightings has resulted in an influx of scientific investigators as well as casual hunters, many armed with lethal weapons, and

WHEREAS, the absence of specific laws covering the taking of specimens encourages laxity in the use of firearms and other deadly devices and poses a clear and present threat to the safety and well-being of persons living or traveling within the boundaries of Skamania County as well as to the creatures themselves,

THEREFORE BE IT RESOLVED that any premeditated, wilful and wanton slaying of any such creature shall be deemed a felony punishable by a fine not to exceed Ten Thousand Dollars ($10,000.00) and/or imprisonment in the county jail for a period not to exceed Five (5) years.

BE IT FURTHER RESOLVED that the situation existing constitutes an emergency and as such this ordinance is effective immediately.

ADOPTED this 1st day of April, 1969.

BOARD OF COMMISSIONERS OF SKAMANIA COUNTY

By _____
              Chairman

APPROVED:

_____
Skamania County Prosecuting Attorney

Establishing the crime of premeditated Sasquatch murder

Although hard to confirm, it appears that there had been some alleged sightings of the creature commonly known as Sasquatch in that area before the ordinance was passed. It should also be noted, however, that the ordinance was adopted on April Fools' Day. On the other hand, the commissioners revisited the issue in 1984, amending the earlier ordinance to declare the county a "Sasquatch Refuge" and to classify Sasquatch killing as a homicide should it be determined that the beast is more man than ape.

That version was passed on April 16.

The 1984 amendment also reduced the penalty for Sasquatch killing, assuming the beast was determined to be more ape than man, to a misdemeanor. This almost certainly reflected doubt as to whether the county board had the power to create new felony offenses, not a desire to encourage Sasquatch killing in any way. If Sasquatch were to be classified as humanoid, then state laws against homicide would apply. Otherwise, the county ordinance would apply, and presumably also state laws against cruelty to animals.

Also of note: the amendment provided that at the trial of any "accused Sasquatch killer," the insanity defense would not be available.

Skamania County, Wash., Ord. 69-01 & 1984-2.[47]

PART SIX

The Laws of States That Are Not the United States or States of the United States

Australian tax commissioners are invested with godlike powers.

It's one thing to turn a blind eye to certain events or declare that they don't count for tax purposes, but in Australia tax commissioners appear to be given fairly complete powers over time and space:

> The Commissioner may:
>   • Treat a particular event that actually happened as not having happened;
>   • Treat a particular event that did not actually happen as having happened and, if appropriate, treat the event as having happened at a particular time and having involved particular action by a particular entity; (or)
>   • Treat a particular event that actually happened as having happened at a time different from the time it actually happened, or having involved particular action by a particular entity (whether or not the event actually involved any action by that entity).

If this works outside Australia there are a couple of presidential administrations I'd like to nullify.

Goods and Services Tax Act § 165.55 (1999).

It's illegal to insult the Minister for Gaming.

At least it is in the Australian state of Victoria, where a 2012 law protects said minister and/or his representative(s) from verbal or other abuse whilst exercising certain duties:

> **3.8.11. Offences relating to obstruction of Minister or**
> **authorised persons**
>   A person must not assault, obstruct, hinder, threaten, abuse,
> insult or intimidate the Minister or an authorised person when
> the Minister or authorised person is exercising or attempting to
> exercise a power under section 3.8.7, 3.8.8, 3.8.9 or 3.8.10.

The other listed sections have to do with inspection of gaming operators' monitoring systems, so this is apparently meant to protect the minister and/or his representatives from being harassed when visiting casinos. It makes sense that it would be illegal to obstruct such an investigation. But it's already illegal to threaten or assault another person (minister or not), so that part of the law is unnecessary. And what drew attention when the bill was introduced was the part making it a crime to "insult . . . the Minister," or at least the opposition was happy to *call* attention to it.

"Is the minister so precious that he now needs legislation to protect him from insults?" said an opposition member, who referred to him as "Windscreens O'Brien" because the bill "proves he's got a glass jaw." (Hey, he's a legislator, not a comedian.) "I thought I better make these comments before the bill passes," he continued, "in case I breach the new rules and insult Mr. O'Brien." Well, unless you do it during an inspection, you can insult him all you want. Even then, I think you'd get away with verbal abuse alone. At least, we consider that a fundamental right in America, although it's in jeopardy these days.

A spokesperson for Windscreens insisted that "[t]he minister can look after himself," but didn't explain why he's specifically mentioned in the law if that's true.

Victoria Gambling Regulation Act 2003, § 3.8.11.

Should the Master in Lunacy be absent, the Deputy Master in Lunacy shall act in his place.

As mentioned earlier, the U.S. Congress only recently eliminated the word "lunatic" from federal law. Australia still uses it, however. Under the Lunacy Act of 1932, the Lunacy Act of 1898 was extended to tiny Norfolk Island, and the appropriate officials appointed:

(1) The Minister may appoint an officer to exercise the powers and perform the functions of Master in Lunacy in Norfolk Island.

(2) There shall be a Deputy Master in Lunacy who shall be appointed by the Minister and shall have and may exercise all the powers and functions of the Master in Lunacy –

  (a) during any absence of the Master in Lunacy from duty or from Norfolk Island;

  (b) during any vacancy in the office of Master in Lunacy; and

  (c) subject to the control and direction of the Master in Lunacy, at any other time.

(3) Where the exercise of a power or function by the Master in Lunacy . . . is dependent upon the opinion, belief or state of mind of the Master in Lunacy in relation to a matter, that power or function may be exercised by the Deputy Master

in Lunacy, or that provision may operate, as the case may be, upon the opinion, belief or state of mind of the Deputy Master in Lunacy in relation to that matter.

You might think the "Master in Lunacy" would be the patient who's been there the longest, but of course it is the title of the official charged with making necessary provisions for . . . well, lunatics.

Lunacy Act 1932; *see also* Lunacy Act 1898 (New South Wales).

The Brazilian stutterers' discount.

In the Brazilian state of Mato Grosso do Sul, cell phone companies are required to give a 50-percent discount to customers who stutter:

> Art. 1º As empresas de telefonia celular instaladas no Estado do Mato Grosso do Sul, deverão conceder 50% (cinqüenta por cento) de desconto em suas tarifas, aos cidadãos portadores de distúrbios na fluência e na temporalização da fala.

Roughly translated:

> Article 1. Cell phone companies installed in the State of Mato Grosso do Sul must provide a 50% (fifty percent) discount on their rates to citizens suffering from disturbances in the timing and fluency of speech.

Presumably, this is to prevent discrimination against people who need twice the number of minutes to finish their conversations.

Note that any citizen claiming the discount must submit the results of an evaluation by a qualified speech therapist, presumably to prevent misuse of the law by unscrupulous nonstutterers.

> Lei No. 3.770, de 4 Novembro de 2009, Diario de Mato Grosso do Sul, de 5.11.2009 (Bra.)

In Canada, they are not amused by attempts to alarm the Queen.

Elizabeth II may no longer be the actual ruler of Canada, but she still has quite a bit of clout there. Or at least I think we can infer that from the fact that attempting to "alarm Her Majesty," or even doing something *intended* to alarm Her Majesty, could get you 14 years in prison:

> Acts intended to alarm Her Majesty or break public peace
> 49. Every one who wilfully, in the presence of Her Majesty,
>   (a) does an act with intent to alarm Her Majesty or to break the public peace, or
>   (b) does an act that is intended or is likely to cause bodily harm to Her Majesty,
>   is guilty of an indictable offence and liable to imprisonment for a term not exceeding fourteen years.

Note that a potentially Queen-alarming act is technically a crime whether or not Her Majesty was *actually* alarmed.

R.S., c. C-34, s. 49 [Criminal Code of Canada].

Beware: margarine served here.

Under the Margarine Act of 1989, public eating places in Nova Scotia must provide the following warning:

> Every keeper of a public eating place where margarine is served shall
> (a) where a menu is used, cause to be displayed thereon in a conspicuous manner the words "margarine is served here";
> (b) where a menu is not used, cause to be displayed in a conspicuous manner in each room or place where food is served a sign or placard bearing the words "margarine is served here" in letters large enough to be distinctly seen from all parts of each room or place.

This appears to be left over from a long war between the forces of butter and an insurrection of margarine supporters. Margarine was actually banned in Canada for most of the period from 1886 until 1948. The federal ban was struck down in 1948 but the war continues in the provinces. Nova Scotia has apparently chosen to protect consumers by requiring signs to alert the public to the presence of margarine and then leaving them to fend for themselves.

At the time this was adopted, it was noted that the supposedly antimargarine measure might actually be good advertising for margarine, but the law remains.

R.S.N.S. c. 269, § 3.[48]

You can't sell cattle without a license, but if you sell cattle, you automatically have a license.

At first glance it seems like this Ontario law creates a problem that it then immediately solves:

Licences

(1) Except under the authority of a licence, no person shall sell cattle.

(2) Every person who sells cattle shall be deemed to be the holder of a licence.

It may be that this is a legislative effort to tax the selling of cattle without using the unpleasant word "tax"—they have just converted it into a licensing fee.

That's the best answer I can come up with, at least.

Beef Cattle Marketing Act, R.S.O. (1990), ch. B.5.3.

Canada frowns upon the crafty sciences.

Like San Francisco (and many other places), Canada is not too keen on those who pretend to have occult powers. But Canada also extends its disapproval to those pretending to apply something called "crafty science":

> 365. Every one who fraudulently
>
> (a) pretends to exercise or to use any kind of witchcraft, sorcery, enchantment or conjuration,
>
> (b) undertakes, for a consideration, to tell fortunes, or
>
> (c) pretends from his skill in or knowledge of an occult or crafty science to discover where or in what manner anything that is supposed to have been stolen or lost may be found,
>
> is guilty of an offence punishable on summary conviction.

Exactly what a "crafty science" (or, for that matter, an "occult science") might be is not clear. The law doesn't define either term and unfortunately no reported cases have grappled with these important questions.

"Crafty" can mean "cunning" or "clever," but given the context here I think we have to assume it's short for "witchcrafty." Ordinarily, a term like "[witch]crafty science" or "occult science" would be an oxymoron, unless you're talking about economics. But here the word "science" is used in the antiquated, pre-Enlightenment sense simply meaning "knowledge" or a particular field of knowledge, verifiable or not. So I think these terms would include the other mentioned items (like fortune-telling) but also reach out to cover similar bullshit like divination, necromancy, reading tea leaves, or whatever.

This breadth might explain why, according to a 2012 *National Post* article, Toronto police use Section 365 "every few months." It appears that the "witchcraft" charges are generally replaced by simple fraud charges, which I imagine are easier to prove these days.

R.S., c. C-34, s. 323 [Criminal Code of Canada].[49]

How to apply for reincarnation.

To the best of my knowledge, a reincarnation permit is required only for Tibetan Buddhists hoping to become a *tulku*, the Tibetan term for "enlightened teacher." The most famous *tulku* (unless you count Steven Seagal, which I don't) is the Dalai Lama, and that might have something to do with the Chinese government's enactment of the following law that requires any "reincarnating living Buddha" to apply for government permission before being reborn:

> Article 1: These measures have been formulated in accordance with the "Regulations on Religious Affairs" in order to guarantee citizens' freedom of religious belief, to respect Tibetan Buddhism's practice of inheriting living Buddha positions, and to regulate the management of living Buddha reincarnation affairs. . . .
>
> Article 5: Reincarnating living Buddhas should carry out application and approval procedures. The application and approval procedure is: the management organization at the monastery applying for the living Buddha reincarnation where the monk is registered, or the local Buddhist Association, should submit applications for reincarnations to the local religious affairs departments [the application is then passed up the chain]. . . .
>
> Article 7: Once an application for a living Buddha's reincarnation has received approval, . . . the corresponding Buddhist Association shall establish a reincarnation guidance team [and] establish a search team to look for the reincarnate soul child. . . .

Article 9: Once a reincarnating living Buddha soul child has been recognized, it shall be reported [for approval]. . . .

Article 10: When the reincarnating living Buddha is installed, a representative of the approving authority shall read out the documents of approval, and the corresponding Buddhist Association shall issue a living Buddha permit. . . .

Article 11: Persons and units who are responsible for being in contravention of these measures and who without authority carry out living Buddha reincarnation affairs, shall be dealt administrative sanction. . . .

Maybe the most comical thing about this one is the claim that the State is regulating Tibetan reincarnation practices in order to guarantee "freedom of religious belief."

State Religious Affairs Bureau Order No. Five (2007).[50]

My swarm of bees has fled! What shall I do?

If you own a bunch of bees (known to bee experts as a "swarm"), and it flies away one day and ends up on somebody else's property, who owns it?

It's too bad they don't teach bee law in school anymore, because this would be a great bar-exam question.

Turns out that the German Civil Code has a set of rules about bee ownership in this situation that seems to cover the gamut of possible outcomes. Most importantly, the first rule of fleeing-bee procedure is that *you must pursue the bees immediately.* Otherwise any claim to swarm ownership will be waived:

> Loss of ownership of bee swarms
>   Where a swarm of bees takes flight, it becomes ownerless if
> the owner fails to pursue it without undue delay or if he gives
> up the pursuit.

Bees are not really considered "domesticated" in the full sense of the word, given that they have a habit of picking up and moving whenever they want to and there isn't much you can do about it, unless you thought ahead and took the time to make a shitload of bee leashes. As is the general rule with captured wild animals, if they get away they are considered to revert back to the wild and to unowned status. As long as you're still pursuing them, though, there is hope.

German Civil Code §§ 960–61.[51]

It flew into my neighbor's empty beehive! Now what?

Let's say your sneaky neighbor, knowing your bees are disgruntled, builds a beehive and leaves the door wide open, hoping they will defect, and they take him up on that offer. What then?

You go get your bees, that's what:

> Right of pursuit of the owner
>
> The owner of the swarm of bees may, in pursuit, enter on plots of land belonging to others. If the swarm has entered an unoccupied beehive belonging to another, the owner of the swarm, for the purpose of capturing it, may open the hive and remove or break out the combs. He must make compensation for the damage caused.

Yep. So long as the hive was empty when they got there, you can break it open and repossess the runaway bees. You'll have to pay for the damage, of course, but that's a small price to pay (depending on the beehive) for getting your bees back and, presumably, teaching them a lesson about loyalty they won't soon forget.

Actually, I wouldn't spend too much time trying to punish a bee, let alone a swarm of bees. That's not going to turn out well.

German Civil Code § 962.

Turns out there were bees in there already! It'll take forever to separate my bees from his!

I have good news and bad news on this one.

The good news is you won't have to try to pick your bees out of a lineup, or worry about any other bee-identification measures. The bad news is that this is because, at least under German bee law, if your bees join up with foreign bees then you lose your rights to the swarm:

> If a bee swarm has moved into an occupied beehive belonging to another, the ownership and the other rights in the bees that were occupying the beehive extend to the swarm that has moved in. The ownership and the other rights in the swarm that has moved in are extinguished.

I guess there needs to be a bright-line rule here of some kind, unless they can get bees to wear little jerseys or something like that to show which team they're on.

German Civil Code § 964.

No, wait! Those are my bees over there! Flying toward that other swarm of bees, which also has someone chasing it! Are you kidding me?

Nein, mein bedauernswerter Imkerfreund. Die Bienenschwärme sind gerade dabei, sich zu vereinigen![52] Now what are you going to do?

Believe it or not, the German Civil Code has a specific statute that is to be applied in the event that two or more swarms flee their hives at approximately the same time and, while properly being pursued by their respective owners in order to preserve their ownership rights, merge to form one larger swarm. Should that happen—and I'd very much like to know if it ever has—the owners split the bees:

> If bee swarms of more than one owner that have moved out merge, the owners who have pursued their swarms become co-owners of the total swarm captured; the shares are determined according to the number of swarms pursued.

So, let's say five swarms are on the move, followed by four bee-keepers flailing around with bee nets (obviously I know nothing about beekeeping). Beekeepers A and B are each pursuing one swarm. C is pursuing two different swarms that tried to flee his place at the same time, while D was just driving by and has never owned a bee in his life.

He just finished beekeeping school, or something. Meanwhile, Beekeeper E is sitting at home not pursuing his swarm, which is one of the five. If all five swarms merge and the resulting *überSchwärm* is captured, what happens?

What happens is that some German lawyers are about to make a bunch of money, that's what happens.

German Civil Code § 963 ("Merging of bee swarms").

In the United Kingdom, part of the Statute of Marlborough is technically still in effect after almost 750 years.

The UK's Law Commission is tasked with reviewing laws and recommending "the repeal of enactments which have been identified, after detailed research and consultation, as being spent, obsolete, unnecessary or otherwise not now of practical utility." According to its 2012 report, four chapters of the Statute of Marlborough—enacted in 1267—were still in effect 745 years later, including this provision:

> In the Year of Grace, One thousand two hundred sixty-seven, the two-and-fiftieth Year of the Reign of King Henry, Son of King John, in the Utas of Saint Martin. . . .
>
> IV. None from henceforth shall cause any Distress that he hath taken, to be driven out of the County where it was [taken]; and if one Neighbour do so to another of his own Authority, and without Judgment, he shall make Fine . . . as for a Thing done against the Peace; nevertheless, if the Lord Presume so to do against his Tenant, he shall be grievously punished by Amerciament. Moreover, Distresses shall be reasonable, and not too great; and he that taketh great and unreasonable Distresses, shall be grievously amerced for the Excess of such Distresses.

The commission found that three of the four chapters were almost but not quite defunct. It was inclined to recommend that the fourth, dealing with the "waste" of property, could safely be repealed. But, it noted, "two individual respondents asserted strongly to us that the tort of waste would be undermined by repeal. . . ." The commission was skeptical but decided there was "room for argument."

Just to be clear, they recommended repealing a law that was 745 years old, and *two people complained*.

Statute of Marlborough 1267 (52 Hen. 3 c.1).[53]

It's still illegal to wear armor in Parliament.

It's been that way since at least 1313:

The King to the Justices of his Bench sendeth Greeting. Whereas of late before certain Persons deputed to treat upon sundry Debates had between Us and certain great Men of our Realm, amongst other things it was accorded, That in our next Parliament after, Provision shall be made by Us, and the common assent of the Prelates, Earls, and Barons, that in all Parliaments, Treatises, and other Assemblies, which should be made in the Realm of England forever, that every Man shall come without all Force and Armour, well and peaceably, to the Honour of Us, and the Peace of Us and our Realm; and now in our next Parliament Prelates, Earls, Barons, and the Commonalty of our Realm, there assembled to take Advice of this Business, have said, that to Us it belongeth, and our part is, through our Royal Seigniory, straitly to defend Force of Armour, and all other Force against our Peace, at all Times when it shall please Us, and to punish them which shall do contrary, according to our Laws and Usages of our Realm; and hereunto they are bound to aid Us as their Sovereign Lord at all Seasons, when need shall be; We command you, that ye cause these Things to be read afore you in the said Bench and there to be enrolled, Given at Westminster, the thirtieth day of October.

It would appear that the King (specifically, Edward II) was forbidding arms as well as armor, assuming that's what he meant by "Force." And that would make sense if the goal was to keep people from fighting (or at least to keep fights from getting serious) in Parliament. To justify this action, the King noted that as the sovereign, to him belongeth a monopoly on the use of force, and also everybody is supposed to do what he says. That's generally the plan, but Edward II wasn't that popular, so he may have felt he needed to remind everybody who was boss.[54]

The Coming Armed to Parliament Act 1313 (7 Edw. 2).

Had Edward II carried a sword instead of a giant stalk of celery, he'd probably have been taken more seriously.

Parliament has taken away the Queen's forests.

In the centuries after the Norman Conquest, the new guys set aside huge tracts of land, especially forests, as royal preserves. Under the "forest law," anyone caught hunting or fishing in the royal forest without permission would be punished. This ticked off a lot of nonroyals, to the extent that there are actually five clauses in the Magna Carta limiting the king's rights to the forest, and a similar "Charter of the Forest" followed a couple of years later.

But the sovereign still had forest rights right up until 1971, when she finally lost them:

> (1) There are hereby abolished—
>
> (a) any prerogative right of Her Majesty to wild creatures (except royal fish and swans), together with any prerogative right to set aside land or water for the breeding, support or taking of wild creatures; and
>
> (b) any franchises of forest, free chase, park or free warren.
>
> (2) The forest law is hereby abrogated, except in so far as it relates to the appointment and functions of verderers.

The 1971 act repealed all or part of three dozen earlier statutes dealing with this royal prerogative, going all the way back to the Charter of the Forest itself.

As we are about to see, however, they did let her keep the swans and royal fish.

Wild Creatures and Forest Laws Act 1971, c. 47.[55]

But she still owns the royal fish.

The Queen's prerogative right to swans and royal fish was expressly preserved by the Wild Creatures and Forest Laws Act 1971, but that law did not address other lingering questions, such as, what exactly is a "royal fish"? Historically, the term referred to whales and sturgeon, part of an ancient royal prerogative codified in 1324 by the statute *De Prerogativa Regis* (you can probably translate that for yourself). Some sources say that the right extends to dolphins and porpoises as well.

This is still the law in England and Wales, as confirmed in 2004 when somebody caught a sturgeon, which was promptly impounded. According to the BBC, Buckingham Palace was contacted and "fairly quickly" responded that the fisherman was welcome to it. That took care of the royal prerogative, but sturgeon are also protected by endangered-species laws, which the Queen can't waive.

In Scotland the responsibility was delegated to the Scottish government in 1999, and the Scots have decided to limit "Royal Fish" to relatively big whales:

> In Scotland 'Royal Fish' are considered to be those stranded whales measuring more than 25 feet from the snout to the middle of the tail.

In a footnote, they explain this is because of a clause in the old statute referring to a "wain [wagon] pulled by six oxen":

> The Scottish Government understands that no stranded whale measuring more than 25 feet from the snout to the middle of the tail could be so drawn to land, and so only intends to review the right to claim stranded whales which measure more than 25 feet from the snout to the middle of the tail.

Again, smaller whales may be protected by other laws, but as far as the Crown is concerned, they're all yours.

De Prerogativa Regis, 17 Edw. II c.11.[56]

No one under 18 may be hypnotized in public.

Under the Hypnotism Act of 1952, unauthorized public hypnotism is banned in the United Kingdom (except for Northern Ireland). A controlling local authority may license or authorize such hypnotism, so long as the person being hypnotized is more than 18 years of age.

> Prohibition on hypnotising persons under twenty-one.
>
> A person who gives an exhibition, demonstration or performance of hypnotism on a person who has not attained the age of eighteen years at or in connection with an entertainment to which the public are admitted, whether on payment or otherwise, shall, unless he had reasonable cause to believe that that person had attained that age, be liable on summary conviction to a fine. . . .

The Act does allow hypnotism for scientific, research, or treatment purposes, but not "in connection with an entertainment."

Hypnotism Act 1952 (1 Eliz. 2 c. 46).

In London, hypnotists must tell subjects not to walk off the stage.

Then there are more specific conditions set forth by local entities, such as the City of London's "Conditions to Be Attached to Licenses for the Performance of Stage Hypnotism." For example, the prospective hypnotist must give his or her real name and address, details of his or her last three performances, and a statement as to whether said hypnotist has been previously convicted of an offense under the Hypnotism Act.

The hypnotist must have insurance, must make a pre-show statement "in a serious manner" telling audience members what to expect and that they can refuse to volunteer. Also,

> a continuous white or yellow line shall be provided on the floor of any raised stage at a safe distance from the edge. This line shall run parallel with the edge of the stage for its whole width. The hypnotist shall inform all subjects that they must not cross the line while under hypnosis, unless specifically told to do so as a part of the performance.

The performance also may not include age regression, consumption of any noxious substance, or "any suggestion that the subject has lost something (e.g., a body part)," the loss of which, "if it really occurred, could cause considerable distress."

Post-hypnotic suggestions are not allowed and must be "completely removed from the minds" of the relevant persons before the performance ends. The hypnotist shall confirm with each subject that they feel well and relaxed; importantly, "the restriction of post-hypnotic suggestions does not prevent the hypnotist telling subjects that they will feel well and relaxed after the suggestions are removed."

Conditions to Be Attached to Licences for the Performance of
Stage Hypnotism, *City of London Ordinances.*

You could get in trouble for causing a nuclear explosion in the UK, too.

Like the other anti-nuke laws we have seen, this law is not really necessary, given that doing this would violate a number of other laws anyway (disturbing the peace comes to mind). But you should know that if you cause a nuclear explosion of any kind in the United Kingdom, they take that very seriously:

> Causing a nuclear explosion.
> (1) Any person who knowingly causes a nuclear weapon test explosion or any other nuclear explosion is guilty of an offence and liable on conviction on indictment to imprisonment for life.
> (2) Nothing in subsection (1) shall apply to a nuclear weapon explosion carried out in the course of an armed conflict.

The purpose of the law is apparently to implement the (not yet ratified) Comprehensive Nuclear Test Ban Treaty. That would explain the exception for attacks that are legal under the law of war, but why a domestic law on this would ever be necessary is not entirely clear. If your side wins one of these conflicts, the losers won't be prosecuting you anyway. If your side loses, prosecution will be the least of your worries. And since it's more likely there won't be anybody left at all, it really won't matter either way.

Note that you can't be convicted under this law unless you *knowingly* cause a nuclear explosion. But all I can say is I hope you have plenty of insurance, because that is some serious negligence, my friend.

Nuclear Explosions (Prohibition and Inspections) Act of 1998, § 1.[57]

How Parliament shortened the titles of its acts.

By passing a series of "Short Titles Acts," of course.

Historically, Acts of Parliament often had titles that were relatively long and descriptive, such as "An Act for preventing tumults and riotous Assemblies, and for the more speedy and effectual punishing the Rioters." Wishing to shorten some titles and standardize others already in use, in 1892 Parliament enacted the first Short Titles Act:

> **An Act to facilitate the Citation of Sundry Acts of Parliament.**
>
> Be it enacted, &c., as follows:
>
> 1.—
>
> > (1.) Each of the acts mentioned in the first schedule to this act may, without prejudice to any other mode of citation, be cited by the short titles therein mentioned in that behalf.
> >
> > (2.) Each of the groups of acts mentioned in the second schedule to this act may . . . be cited by the collective title therein mentioned in that behalf. . . .
>
> 2. This act may be cited as the Short Titles Act, 1892.

Note that rather than giving the Short Titles Act a short title to begin with, they gave it a long title and then made it the first act to have its title shortened by itself.

The effects were dramatic in other cases as well; for example, the long title quoted above became simply "The Riot Act." Actually, this

THE RIOT ACT.

If any persons to the number of 12 or more unlawfully, riotously, and tumultuously assemble together to the disturbance of the public peace and being required by any Justice by proclamation in the King's name in the exact form of the Riot Act, I George I, Sess. 2 c. 5 s. 2, to disperse themselves and peaceably depart, shall to the number of 12 or more unlawfully, riotously and tumultuously remain or continue together for an hour after such proclamation shall be guilty of a felony.

The Form of Proclamation is as follows :—

"Our Sovereign Lord the King chargeth and commandeth all persons, being assembled, immediately to disperse themselves, and peaceably depart to their habitations, or to their lawful business, upon the pains contained in the Act made in the first year of King George the First for preventing tumults and riotous assemblies."

GOD SAVE THE KING.

It came in this handy booklet for easier reading.

may not have saved much time, because they still had to read rioters the rest of the Riot Act anyway.

Other Short Titles Acts followed. More recently, the Statute Law Revision Act 2012 provided that the Short Titles Acts from 1896 forward, along with certain other provisions, could be cited collectively as the "Short Titles Acts 1896 to 2012," thus shortening the titles of multiple Short Titles Acts in a single stroke.

Short Titles Act 1892 (long version), 55 & 56 Vict. c.10.

No person shall interfere with a fungus.

A British regulation limits the sorts of things people can do in nearly two dozen areas including Hyde Park, Kensington Gardens, and Greenwich Park, at least without written permission. For example:

[N]o person using a Park shall—
  (1) interfere with any plant or fungus;
  (2) go on any flower bed or shrubbery. . . ;
  (3) use or operate a metal or mineral detector or any device for locating objects below ground level;
  (4) attach any article to, climb or interfere with any tree, railing, fence, statue, seat, building or structure;
  (5) interfere with any notice or sign. . . ;
  (9) play or cause to be played a musical instrument. . . ;
  (11) [p]roject any missile manually or by artificial means;
  (12) camp or erect or cause to be erected any tent or enclosure;
  (13) wash or dry any piece of clothing or linen. . . ;
  (15) make or give a public speech or address except in the public speaking area in Hyde Park. . . ;
  (18) take photographs of still or moving subjects [for professional purposes]. . . ;
  (20) fish, take any egg, or intentionally injure or worry any animal or bird. . . ; [or]
  (24) feed or touch any deer or pelican. . . .

How one might "interfere with a fungus," or even determine what said fungus is up to for purposes of interfering with that activity, is not explained.

The Royal Parks and Other Open Spaces Regulations 1997, 1997 No. 1639
(effective 1 Oct. 1997, as amended).

Come to my aid, my prince, for someone does me wrong.

On the islands of Jersey and Guernsey in the English Channel, if you see another person committing a civil offense you can force that person to stop what he or she is doing by means of the following procedure:

- → Ensure there are witnesses about;
- → Drop to your knees and raise one hand in the air;
- → Shout *Haro! Haro! Haro! A l'aide, mon Prince, on me fait tort!*
- → Problem solved.

This is the *Clameur de Haro*, believed to be almost 1,000 years old and still in effect today. It means, very roughly: "Hear me! Hear me! Hear me! Come to my aid, my Prince, for someone does me wrong!" Basically, it is a sort of self-help temporary restraining order; once the *clameur* has been uttered, the alleged wrongdoer must stop until the dispute can be heard by a court.

This is a common-law tradition but it does appear in Jersey's written court rules, so I'm including it here:

(1) The fines imposed by the Court in matters of Clameur de Haro or of contempt thereof shall be in the discretion of the Court.

(2) Actions resulting from the raising of the Clameur de Haro shall be instituted in conjunction with the Attorney General and shall be dealt with as causes de brièveté.

As you can see, you can be fined for "contempt of clameur," which could mean either clameuring inappropriately or failing to heed a clameur.

Jersey Royal Court Rules 10/4.[58]

Papua New Guinea has repealed the Sorcery Act.

It could be argued that Papua New Guinea's Sorcery Act 1971 was the rough equivalent of the laws against fortune-telling and similar practices that exist in other countries (and are mentioned above), but the Sorcery Act was much more comprehensive than those laws. And while the Act declared that it was not saying sorcery was real, it seemed to walk much closer to that line than similar laws elsewhere:

> There is no reason why a person who uses or pretends or tries to use sorcery to do, or to try to do, evil things should not be punished just as if sorcery and the powers of sorcerers were real, since it is just as evil to do or to try to do evil things by sorcery as it would be to do them, or to try to do them, in any other way.
>
> * * *
>
> Even though this Act may speak as if powers of sorcery really exist (which is necessary if the law is to deal adequately with all the legal problems of sorcery and the traditional belief in the powers of sorcerers), nevertheless nothing in this Act recognizes the existence or effectiveness of powers of sorcery in any factual sense except only for the purpose of, and of proceedings under or by virtue of, this Act, or denies the existence or effectiveness of such powers.

One major problem: the Act distinguished between "forbidden" and "innocent" sorcery, and the "burden of proof that an act of sorcery is an act of innocent sorcery is on the person alleging it."

Happily, the legislature repealed the Sorcery Act in 2013. A number of people suspected of being sorcerers had been murdered, causing lawmakers to think maybe the law was not sending quite the right message.

Sorcery Act 1971, Preamble & § 5.[59]

Chewing gum is a controlled substance in Singapore.

Will you be caned for chewing gum in Singapore? The answer appears to be no. Contrary to popular belief, it is not illegal to chew gum in Singapore — with one important exception — if you can find any. But it is illegal to import, mail, sell, or advertise it there, so that may not be easy.

Gum has been largely banned since 1992, in an effort to keep the streets clean and stop unidentified morons from sticking wads of it on the door sensors of railway cars. Transit regulations make it illegal to "consume or attempt to consume" any gum on railway premises, but otherwise I found no law against chewing or possessing the stuff.

But you can't buy it in Singapore, nor can it be imported. Gum is allowed to pass through, but only in a sealed convoy, as if it were a load of plutonium or something:

> 5. A person who imports chewing gum into Singapore in transit to or from West Malaysia shall —
>
> > (a) ensure that chewing gum in transit by road is conveyed in a container or in completely covered vehicles or wagons which are capable of being locked, sealed or otherwise secured;
> >
> > (b) upon importation, lock, seal or otherwise secure the consignment of chewing gum . . . ;
> >
> > (c) arrange, at his own expense, for the consignment of chewing gum to be escorted to [or from the free trade zone; and]

(d) submit to the Director-General the export permit for the
re-export of the chewing gum within 7 days.

Note that it's not illegal to *manufacture* gum. In 2013, a German company said it would open a facility there to make the "food-grade rubber" that is the basis of gum, which will arguably make gum-hating Singapore one of the world's main sources of it.

See Singapore Sale of Food (Prohibition of Chewing Gum) Regulations;
Regulation of Imports and Exports (Chewing Gum) Regulations.[60]

The Swiss respect the "dignity" of plant life.

Well, they're thinking about it, anyway.

Switzerland's federal constitution contains this provision:

> Der Bund erlässt Vorschriften über den Umgang mit Keim- und
> Erbgut von Tieren, Pflanzen und anderen Organismen. Er trägt
> dabei der Würde der Kreatur sowie der Sicherheit von Mensch,
> Tier und Umwelt Rechnung und schützt die genetische Vielfalt
> der Tier- und Pflanzenarten.

Or, in the (nonofficial) English translation:

> The Confederation shall legislate on the use of reproductive and
> genetic material from animals, plants and other organisms. In
> doing so, it shall take account of the dignity of living beings as
> well as the safety of human beings, animals and the environ-
> ment, and shall protect the genetic diversity of animal and plant
> species.

In 2008, a Swiss committee issued a report based on its view that
the legal term "dignity of living beings" (Würde der Kreatur) required
a consideration of the ethical and moral duties owed to plants, if any.
Should der Pflanzen be protected "for their own sake," or only because
they are useful to der Mensch?

The committee considered this carefully, taking on questions like
whether plants are sentient (only a "small group" considered that plau-

sible) and whether a plant could be said to have a "goal" or "purpose" that deserves respect.

Not surprisingly, the committee didn't reach any clear answers. In fact, the only unanimous conclusion was that it is "morally impermissible" to inflict arbitrary harm on plants, such as the "decapitation of wild flowers . . . without rational reason." Technically, the constitution seems to *require* only considering plant dignity when legislating on genetic issues, so if you enjoy decapitating wild flowers for no good reason, you're not a criminal, just a bad person.

Swiss Fed. Const. art. 120, § 2.[61]

Sources and Bibliography

In addition to the relevant legal codes themselves, I consulted many sources when trying to locate and verify the laws mentioned in this book. It is hard to imagine having completed this project without the Internet, so thanks to whoever came up with that. I visited far too many websites to list, including the official sites of all 50 U.S. state legislatures, the U.S. Government Printing Office, the U.K. National Archives' excellent Legislation.gov.uk site, and many official sites in other nations as well. Other sources are cited in the endnotes.

Some physically printed books I consulted by going to the "library" include the following:

Drew, Katherine Fischer, *The Laws of the Salian Franks* (University of Pennsylvania Press, 1991).

Feldbrugge, Ferdinand, *Law in Medieval Russia* (Leiden, the Netherlands: Koninklijke Brill NV, 2009).

Henderson, Ernest F. , *Select Historical Documents of the Middle Ages* (London: George Bell & Sons, 1910).

Hoffner, Harry Angier, Jr., *The Laws of the Hittites: A Critical Edition* (Leiden, the Netherlands: Koninklijke Brill NV, 1997), and chapter 12 of Law Collections (also contributed by Hoffner).

Johns, C.H.W. , M.A. (translator), *The Oldest Code of Laws in the World* (Edinburgh: T. & T. Clark, 1926).

Johnson, Allan Chester, Paul Robinson Coleman-Norton, and Frank Card Bourne, *Ancient Roman Statutes: A Translation* (Univ. of Texas Press, 1961).

Kaiser, Daniel H. , *The Growth of the Law in Medieval Russia* (Princeton University Press, 1980).

Roth, Martha T. , *Law Collections from Mesopotamia and Asia Minor*, 2d ed. (Atlanta: Scholars Press, 1997).

Watson, Alan, *Ancient Law and Modern Understanding: At the Edges* (Univ. of Georgia Press, 1998) (especially chapter six, "On Gathering Acorns").

Westbrook, Raymond, ed., *A History of Ancient Near Eastern Law* (Leiden, the Netherlands: Koninklijke Brill NV, 2003).

Nathan Belofsky also deserves credit for making what is, to my knowledge, the only other comprehensive attempt to verify the laws discussed in any "dumb laws" book or website:

Belofsky, Nathan, *The Book of Strange and Curious Legal Oddities* (Perigee Books, 2010).

Acknowledgments/Credits

I would like to thank the readers of *Lowering the Bar* generally, and in particular those who contributed strange or stupid laws for use in this book or otherwise helped in its creation. I couldn't have done it without you, which should be interpreted as a figure of speech meaning sincere appreciation rather than an actual admission of inability to complete the project without assistance, but it is at least true that I'd probably never have found some of the items included here without your help. I sincerely appreciate it. Some who contacted me did not use their real name, which is completely understandable, and of course I may just have missed some people, for which I apologize. In any event, known contributors include (but are not necessarily limited to):

Justice William Bedsworth
Ryan Caldwell
Matthew Caplan
John Cotter
Joanna Delany
Katharina Doll
Emily B. C. Durham
Avi Efreom
Randy Evers
Marcos Exposto
Jesse Fettkether
Andrew Gray
Tom Harrison
Ian Hay
Sebastian Hoeges
Charles Ivey IV

Adam Jacobs
Blake Kirk
David Kramer
Jonathan Leblang
Daniel Libman
Howard Mann
Louise Park
Ron Parker
Ken Parkinson
Eric Ryan
Gary Slapper
John Stracke
Michael Sweeney
Mark Thorson
Jason Tree
Adolph Voigt

My cuneiform skills are a little rusty, so I had to rely on others for translation. Thanks to Daniel A. Foxvog of UC Berkeley for permission to use his translation of the Urukagina reform edict. I found the translation at Jerald Starr's fascinating website, sumerianshakespeare .com.

Material from *Ancient Roman Statutes* is reprinted by permission of The University of Texas Press.

Special thanks to Sharon Ball of New Mexico's Legislative Council Service for digging up an actual copy of the 1995 wizard bill, and to Sally Harlow of the Texas Legislative Reference Library for unearthing the 1971 resolution "honoring" the Boston Strangler.

Thanks to law clerk/associate Edd Gaus for checking the citations, which I know was just the kind of exciting experience he imagined having during those seven long years of law school. Any errors in this book, of course, are entirely Edd's responsibility.

I would also like to thank Tom Giesler, a professional patent illustrator who bravely agreed to take on the mind-numbing task of reading a 316-word definition of "buttocks" and then attempting to sketch it out for this book. I think the result is a great success and will provide important guidance to city officials and buttock owners across the land.

Finally, I would like to dedicate this book to my family. They are wonderful people who I love dearly and who deserve much of the credit—but none of the blame—for everything I do.

Image Credits

Urukugina fragment: item is in the Louvre; photo by Marie Lan-Nguyen (via Wikipedia). Hammurabi stela: also in the Louvre; photo by Claude Vallette (via flickr). Map of Mesopotamia: from L.W. King's *A History of Sumer and Akkad*. Athenian jury ballots: Sharon Mollerus (via flickr). Peter the Great's "beard token": America.gov (accompanied an article about coins in the Smithsonian's collection). Richard I vs. Saladin at the Battle of Arsuf: Gustave Doré. The "feeble-mindedness" pie chart: Louis E. Bisch, "Nearly 15,000,000 School Children Are Defectives," *New York Times*, p. SM 10 (Sept. 28, 1913). Horrifying scorpion: Michael L. Baird (via flickr), flickr.bairdphotos.com. Mushroom cloud: A 1955 test that was part of "Operation Teapot"; photo courtesy of National Nuclear Security Administration/Nevada Field Office. The bolo tie: Jessa Dow-Anderson, Different Seasons Jewelry (via flickr). The Boy Scout cavalry troop: photo from the Bain Collection at the Library of Congress, date unknown. The "punt gun": from the National Photo Company collection at the Library of Congress. Mongoose delinquents: Dave Lau (via flickr). "To Square the Circle": image is an article in the *Indianapolis Sentinel* (Jan. 20, 1897), found via Google's news archive. New Mexico's wizard bill: image of a PDF provided to the author by the New Mexico Legislative Council Service. Resolution honoring Albert DeSalvo: image of a PDF provided to the author by the Texas Legislative Reference Library. Foot x-ray machine: U.S. Patent Office. The buttocks schematic: an original work created by patent illustrator Tom Giesler specifically for this book, believe it or not. The emergency Sasquatch ordinance: both ordinances are available on Skamania County's website. Edward II: from a manuscript in the British Library (Royal MS 20 A II [F.10]). The Riot Act: public-domain image of a booklet used in the early 20th century (via Wikipedia).

Endnotes

1. The quotations given here are from the 1915 translation by L.W. King, the text of which is available at the website of Yale Law School's Avalon Project.

2. These laws are often referred to, at least on the Internet, as the "Code of the Nesilim," but no actual Hittite scholars seem to call them that. Nesili was apparently the language that the dominant group spoke at the time, so they are sometimes called the Nesilim. But the scholars call this collection the Laws of the Hittites, so that's what I've used here.

3. On the subject of which animals to stay away from, see also *Leviticus* 18–20 and *Deuteronomy* 22.

4. The date of 725 B.C. is an arbitrary point I selected within the dates that Romulus is supposed to have ruled (753–716 B.C.), not when these laws would have been written down. For that matter, people might have ascribed this work to Romulus or one of the other seven kings even if it was a later development, just because they didn't know the actual date. People do things like that, you know.

5. Quotations are from the translation by Sir Frederic G. Kenyon. Since his work was published, archaeologists have found actual ballots in Athens and it turns out they were disks, not "balls," as Kenyon had written.

6. *See* ARISTOPHANES, THE CLOUDS 497–99. Plato also mentions it in the LAWS (Book XII, ¶ 7), but Plato did not even pretend to be a comedian.

7. The quote by Cicero appears in Book Two of *De Legibus*, in which he depicts himself engaging in the same sort of dialogue that Socrates had 350 years before, lecturing and greatly impressing his listeners with his education and impeccable logic. Coincidentally, Cicero was also eventually executed.

8. *See* KATHERINE FISCHER DREW, THE LAWS OF THE SALIAN FRANKS 82–83 (1991). The Salic law is mentioned by Shakespeare in *Henry V* (act I, scene ii), although the issue there had to do with succession rights — specifically, who had a valid claim to France — not jumping over fences. The law was apparently first codified around 507–511, but was around for quite a while, which explains the date of 650 in the text. The fact that Henry V was still worrying about it in 1415 shows how long legal customs can last. (In the play, the English decide Salic law doesn't apply, which coincidentally meant that Henry's claim was better. If they had agreed with the French argument, of course, it would have been a pretty boring play.)

9. Some scholars have suggested that the reason for the disparity in fines was that the payment was more to compensate for injuries to honor and dignity rather than for economic or material harm. I guess having someone pull your beard out could be considered more embarrassing than having him cut off a finger, but fingers don't grow back.

10. The edict is reprinted in ERNEST F. HENDERSON, SELECT HISTORICAL DOCUMENTS OF THE MIDDLE AGES (1910). *See also* THE LATER CRUSADES, 1189–1311, 56 (R.L. Wolff & H.W. Hazard eds., 1969) (saying that Richard issued his rules for the Crusade fleet in June 1190, and that the "severe, almost savage, ordinances" didn't stop some crusaders from raping and pillaging Lisbon when they stopped there on the way to the Holy Land).

11. *See House Approves Eliminating 'Lunatic' From Federal Law*, N.Y. TIMES, p. A21, Dec. 6, 2012.

12. *See* Anderson v. Dunn, 19 U.S. 204, 224–35 (1821) (recognizing the implied contempt power); Watkins v. United States, 354 U.S. 178, 195–216 (1957) (vacating conviction of a witness who refused

to answer questions from the House Committee on Un-American Activities); 11 Stat. 155–56 (1857) (the original contempt statute). According to one scholar, Congress locked people up for contempt at least 85 times between 1795 and 1934. DAVID SWANSON, DAYBREAK: UNDOING THE IMPERIAL PRESIDENCY AND FORMING A MORE PERFECT UNION 136–39 (2009). The issue of how and where it did this was raised again in 2007 by some people interested in finding the "Congressional jail" and throwing certain Bush administration officials in it. *Id.*; *see also* Adam Cohen, *Congress Has a Way of Making Witnesses Speak: Its Own Jail*, N.Y. TIMES, Dec. 4, 2007. According to Swanson, though, Congress has never actually had "its own jail," although it has used the jail in the District of Columbia, which it governs directly.

13. The details of live-scorpion mailing are taken from U.S. Postal Service Publication 52 on hazardous and restricted mail. Scorpions are mailed for research purposes and for making anti-venom, and occasionally as a gift to the in-laws. The law also says you can't mail "infernal machines," which is a fun term for bombs. The term reportedly dates back to 1800, when Napoleon narrowly missed being assassinated by a time bomb, which he angrily called a *machine infernale.* It was later applied to other kinds of bombs that could be set to blow up automatically. CHARLES GANNON, RUMORS OF WAR AND INFERNAL MACHINES 1 (2003).

14. Jones v. United States, 137 U.S. 202 (1890).

15. Fillmore's speech:

> Peruvian guano has become so desirable an article to the agricultural interest of the United States that it is the duty of the Government to employ all the means properly in its power for the purpose of causing that article to be imported into the country at a reasonable price. Nothing will be omitted on my part toward accomplishing this desirable end.

> Brave words of leadership, Millard. Strange that you are consistently ranked as one of the five worst presidents ever.

16. At least prior to this law, there was an argument that the highest-ranking American general ever was John J. Pershing, commander of U.S. forces in World War I. The bicentennial declaration has probably settled that in Washington's favor, but you know what? They're both winners in my book.

17. Allie Bidwell, "One Civil War Veteran's Pension Remains on Government's Payroll," *U.S. News and World Report* (July 3, 2013).

18. The relevant U.K. law is the Public Order Act 1986.

19. Laser-pointer laws of this kind are not uncommon, and here's a definition that would exclude flashlights: "As used in this section, 'laser' means a device that utilizes the natural oscillations of atoms or molecules between energy levels for generating coherent electromagnetic radiation in the ultraviolet, visible, or infrared region of the spectrum, and when discharged exceeds one milliwatt continuous wave." CAL. PEN. CODE § 247.5. See? Not so hard.

20. On that same momentous day, the Texas Legislature passed H.R. Con. Res. 25, designating Friona, Texas, as the state's official Cheeseburger Capital.

21. These comic books were apparently second only to communism in the threat posed to the American way of life. "The subcommittee believes that this Nation cannot afford the calculated risk involved in the continued mass dissemination of crime and horror comic books to children." SENATE COMMITTEE ON THE JUDICIARY, COMIC BOOKS AND JUVENILE DELINQUENCY, Interim Rep. (1955). Only the voluntary Comics Code saved the Republic.

22. Reed v. King, 145 Cal. App. 3d 261 (1983).

23. The only person who's tried out the statute since it was passed was a woman who cited it when criticizing someone for talking to the papers about a murder that had taken place in the house. She would probably have lost anyway, but the fact that she was the one who committed the murder probably didn't help.

24. Weiner v. City of San Diego, 229 Cal. App. 3d 1203, 1211 n.4 (1991).

25. The quote about the unyielding grizzly bear comes from "California in Time: From the War with Mexico to Statehood," a document

that can be found on the website of the California Department of Parks and Recreation. The bear had been a California symbol since at least 1846, when it appeared on the first flag of the California Republic. This was a handmade flag painted with blackberry juice, and the artwork left something to be desired. Contemporary accounts make clear that the animal was intended to be a grizzly bear, but as noted by Mariano Guadalupe Vallejo in his memoirs, "the bear was so badly painted . . . that it looked more like a pig than a bear." MARIANO GUADALUPE VALLEJO, HISTORICAL AND PERSONAL MEMOIRS RELATING TO ALTA CALIFORNIA [RECUERDOS HISTORICOS Y PERSONALES TOCANTE A LA ALTA CALIFORNIA], Vol. 5: 1845–48, 87–90, 93–98, 101–103, 106–107 (Earl R. Hewitt trans., 1875) (reprinted at www.historymatters.gmu.edu).

26. *In re* Anthony J., 72 Cal. App. 4th 1326 (1999).

27. The trial judge in Anthony's case decided the proper charge was aiding and abetting a lynching (his own), which the Court of Appeal found "understandable; it is awkward to apply the definition provided in section 405a to hold that a person can 'take' himself from police custody." But it held that wasn't necessary, since 405b punishes "every person" who participates in a lynching.

28. New Mexico v. Colorado, 267 U.S. 30 (1925).

29. *See* People *ex rel.* Flanders v. Neary, 154 P.2d 48 (1944); People *ex rel.* Past v. Owers, 69 P. 515 (1902).

30. In the King James version, at least, fire and brimstone are mentioned together (although that specific phrase is not always used) 12 times: in *Genesis* 19:24 (Sodom and Gomorrah); *Psalms* 11:6; *Isaiah* 30:33 (describing the Lord's breath as "like a stream of brimstone," which doesn't seem very nice); *Ezekiel* 38:22; *Luke* 17:29 (Sodom again); and *Revelation* 9:17 (twice), 9:18, 14:10, 19:20, 20:10, and 21:8. Squirrels are not mentioned at all.

31. Many states have antimilitia laws of this kind, and while the motivation (controlling hate groups) is a good one, there is reason to question whether these laws are constitutional. The First Amendment protects the right to associate, and the Second Amendment protects the "right to bear arms," so it's not exactly a stretch to

say the Constitution protects the right to associate while bearing arms. But at least one court has upheld a law of this kind, though the court construed the law narrowly in order to say it permissibly regulated conduct and not just speech or association. Vietnamese Fisherman's Ass'n v. Knight Riders of the Ku Klux Klan, 543 F. Supp. 198 (S.D. Tex. 1982). It remains to be seen what would happen in a case that didn't involve a bunch of Klansmen. Some arguably reasonable people have suggested it might one day take "a militia amounting to near half a million of citizens with arms in their hands" to guarantee that the federal government doesn't get out of control. JAMES MADISON, THE FEDERALIST NO. 46 (1788). On the other hand, what did James Madison know about the Constitu. . . . Oh. Right.

32. Haslem v. Lockwood, 37 Conn. 500 (1871); Church v. Meeker, 34 Conn. 421 (1867). In *Church*, the landowner had hired a guy who lived in a shanty on the beach to make the heaps. When Meeker showed up to take some, "the occupant of the shanty forbade him. The defendant thereupon gave him ten cents and he made no further objection."

33. A tongue-in-cheek amendment was offered that would have named the bill the "Jim Norman Animal Paparazzi Protection Act," but it was later withdrawn.

34. Two hundred years later, Justice Thurgood Marshall discussed the "benefit of clergy" doctrine in the course of explaining why he agreed that the death penalty was unconstitutional. Furman v. Georgia, 408 U.S. 238, 334 n.47 (1972) (Marshall, J., concurring) (citing H. BEDAU, THE DEATH PENALTY IN AMERICA). (The Court changed its mind four years later.) The doctrine technically may still be the law in jurisdictions that haven't specifically abolished it, but if your defense attorney is advising you to give it a shot for that reason, you should know that you are probably screwed.

35. The island of Kauai had been free of the mongoose scourge, but in 2012 the *New York Times* reported that one of the little bastards had been trapped there (on Kauai, not at the *Times*). Rachel Newer, *An Invader Advances in Hawaii*, N.Y. TIMES, June 11,

2012. Nobody knows how they got there or how many there may be. But if you see one, you can kill it and they'll probably give you a medal or something.

36. Indiana House Journal, 1897, at pp. 199, 213, 489, 588-89; *see* Justin E. Walsh, *The Centennial History of the Indiana General Assembly, 1816-1978*, at pp. 428-29 (Indianapolis 1987). For contemporary reports, *see* To Square the Circle, INDIANAPOLIS SENTINEL, Jan. 20, 1897, at p. 5, and *The Mathematical Bill*, INDIANAPOLIS NEWS, Feb. 13, 1897, at p. 11 (reporting that the House bill "was brought up and made fun of" in the Senate). For math stuff, *see* David Singmaster, "The Legal Values of Pi," *in* PI: A SOURCE BOOK 236 (J.L. Berggren et al. eds., 2004), and P. Beckmann, A HISTORY OF PI, at pp. 170-73 (Boulder 1970).

37. The wizard-bill incident was mentioned in a variety of newspapers at the time, generally being cited as evidence that there was something wrong with our system of representative government. *See, e.g., Poll Shows Legislators Don't Have Many Fans*, SANTA FE NEW MEXICAN, Mar. 6, 1995; *Going Insane in Cleveland and Other Places*, ALBUQUERQUE JOURNAL, July 2, 1996. There is something very wrong with that system, but this isn't it. I mean, have you seen some of the other stuff our legislatures spew out? (Have you read the rest of this book, for example? If not, why did you start here?) This is one of the things that actually gives me some hope.

38. As of the date of writing, the post mentioned could be found in the "general discussion" section of the forums at the website www.ssnakess.com.

39. *See* Asma Khalid, "A Whole Lot Of Hollerin' To Save A Dying Art," *National Public Radio* (June 18, 2012), *available at* npr.org.

40. The church first renounced plural marriage in 1890, when its president issued a manifesto declaring that Mormons would "refrain from contracting any marriage forbidden by the law of the land," a position the church membership then formally adopted. But evidence turned up that not everybody was on board with this. That led to a second manifesto in 1904, not coincidentally while

Congress was holding hearings into whether Smoot should be
allowed to serve as a Utah senator. He was, and served for many
years. Other than this controversy, he is probably best known for
cosponsoring legislation that created the National Park Service,
which is great, and the Smoot-Hawley Tariff Act, which sucked.

41. *See* Patrick T. Reardon, "The Highway Is Their Home," *Chicago
Tribune* (Mar. 17, 2000) (noting that the group's largest settled
community is in Murphy Village, South Carolina).

42. The U.S. Supreme Court has held that state attempts to regulate
private sexual conduct between consenting adults are unconstitutional—as long as no money changes hands, at least. *Lawrence
v. Texas*, 539 U.S. 558 (2003) (striking down ban on "sodomy").
That would seem to answer the question whether this Texas law
is enforceable.

43. *See House 'Honors' Boston Strangler*, AUSTIN AMERICAN, Apr. 2,
1971 (reporting that the resolution "passed without dissent during routine House business"). The resolution was introduced by
Rep. Tom Moore Jr., who withdrew it after it passed, "bringing
chuckles from several of his colleagues" who were in on the joke.
Moore insisted it was only a joke, but another representative tried
to make more out of it. "It just proves you could pass anything in
the House," he said. Interestingly, although a copy of the measure
is in the legislature's files, there is no record of it in the legislative
journal for that day, or in any of the other sources where official
measures are recorded. (The number of the resolution is actually
"unknown"—it was never given a number.) I wanted to be sure to
include a copy here in case the original also mysteriously vanishes.
By the way, although there was no solid evidence in 1967 proving
DeSalvo was the Boston Strangler, DNA testing reportedly linked
him to those crimes in 2013.

44. The St. Johns ordinance was upheld in 1995. *See Café 207, Inc. v.
St. Johns County*, 856 F. Supp. 641 (M.D. Fla. 1994); *aff'd*, 66 F.3d
272 (11th Cir. 1995) (adopting district court's reasoning). Note
that the word count given here does not count the word being
defined, the concluding summary sentence, or a sentence at the

beginning that informs readers that they will find such a summary if they can actually make it to the end. In my view, those are not properly part of the buttocks definition *per se*. As noted, many other local governments have followed St. Johns' lead since the court ruling. The town that got it wrong is McHenry, Illinois. *See* McHenry, Ill., Mun. Code § 2.50-1 (2012). It's not too surprising that nobody has ever noticed this error (until now), since it is obscured by all the ridiculous verbiage.

45. *See* Robbie Brown, *Arkansas Town Draws a Line on Clubs*, N.Y. TIMES, July 19, 2011. In written reports, the mayor wondered sarcastically whether Arkansas was "still part of America." Assuming he meant the United States, Arkansas has in fact been part of America since 1803, except for 1861 to 1865, when it technically wasn't.

46. The 2011 bill was introduced by the Castro District's own representative, who said nudity was fine as long as people were decent about it. "It used to be that there would be one nude guy wandering around the neighborhood and no one thought twice about it," he said. "Now it's a regular thing and much more obnoxious. We have guys sitting down naked in public without the common decency to put something down underneath them." Yep, it's those guys that ruin it for everybody else.

47. At least one other Washington county has also declared itself a "Sasquatch protection and refuge area." Whatcom County, Wash., Res. 1992-043. Whatcom is at the other end of the state, however, so until other counties follow suit the Sasquatch will remain unable to travel between the two refuges. It may be, of course, that these are two entirely separate Sasquatch populations to begin with. Further study is clearly needed.

48. The definitive account of the Canadian Margarine Wars is almost certainly W.H. HEICK, A PROPENSITY TO PROTECT: BUTTER, MARGARINE AND THE RISE OF URBAN CULTURE IN CANADA (Wilfrid Laurier Univ. Press 1991).

49. *See* Tristin Hopper, *Canada's witch trials: Fake sorcerers and sham psychics abound despite hundred-year-old law to protect people,*

NATIONAL POST (Dec. 10, 2012). Hopper mentions a 2009 case in which someone was charged under Section 365 for allegedly defrauding a victim out of $100,000, said victim being a lawyer, who really should have known better.

50. *See* "Measures on the Management of the Reincarnation of Living Buddhas in Tibetan Buddhism," translated by the International Campaign for Tibet and posted by the U.S. Congressional-Executive Commission on China (*http://www.cecc.gov*). The original text is available at the website of the State Administration of Religious Affairs (*http://www.sara.gov.cn*).

51. Bee laws are not new by any means. In fact, there is a reference to bee swarms in the Laws of the Hittites, which as you may recall date back to around 1750 B.C. Section 91 and 92 of those laws don't say anything about mixing swarms, but they do impose a five-shekel penalty for stealing one.

52. "Oh, no, my unfortunate beekeeping friend. The swarms will merge!" Or at least that's the translation my source gave me.

53. This thing is so old that one of its original purposes was to reconfirm the Magna Carta, for God's sake, and its original text was not in modern English. You can read a translation and see an image of the original at www.legislation.gov.uk/aep/Hen3cc1415/52/1 (last visited Aug. 21, 2013).

54. This statute also was not originally in modern English. Like the Statute of Marlborough, it appears to have been in what is sometimes called Anglo-Norman French. The Normans brought their dialect of French along in 1066 and Anglo-Norman French was used for legal and administrative purposes for centuries. (It hangs around even today in terms like "court-martial.") What is given here is said to be the "traditional translation" of the Act.

55. Historically, tree-infested areas were known as woods, and the term "forest" referred only to wooded areas that belonged to the Crown. That's why all the statutes mentioned in this item are called forest laws or forest charters.

56. *See Police inquiry over sturgeon sale*, BBC NEWS (June 3, 2004). Interestingly, when the Law Commission (the group that reviews

U.K. laws and recommends obsolete laws for repeal) issued its report on the forest laws and other old royal prerogatives, it noted that "[t]he Queen has indicated that she no longer wishes to retain this right in the case of whales and sturgeons." But as shown in the text, the law that resulted in 1971 did not take that right away. It seems unlikely that she suddenly developed an interest in beached whales and so changed her mind about giving them up, but I haven't been able to find a reason why Parliament wanted her to keep them.

57. New Zealand has a similar law, but the punishment is much more lenient, with a maximum of 10 years in jail or a fine of up to NZ$1 million. New Zealand Nuclear-Test-Ban Act 1999, §§ 5 & 6. I'm not suggesting you choose New Zealand for nuclear-testing purposes, I'm just pointing this out.

58. Jersey and Guernsey (and the other small islands in those bailiwicks) are just off the French coast and were historically part of the Duchy of Normandy. The English monarchy lost Normandy itself but kept the Channel Islands, which today are still British "crown dependencies" technically owned directly by the sovereign, and are not part of the United Kingdom itself. These days they are largely self-governing, which is part of the reason they still have this *haro* thing. *See generally* V. Carey, *The Clameur de Haro,* 11 GUERNSEY L.J. 31–35 (1991).

59. Interestingly, the Sorcery Act makes it "a defense to a charge of adultery that an act of sorcery had been performed," without the consent of the adulterer, "of such a nature as to be generally believed, in the social groups of which the husband and wife are respectively members, to have the effect . . . of inducing the accused person to have the sexual intercourse in question. . . ." Papua New Guinea Sorcery Act 1971, § 15.

60. There is also an exception for certain "chewing gum with therapeutic value," an exception that resulted after heavy lobbying by Wrigley, connected with the negotiation of a 2004 free-trade agreement between the United States and Singapore.

61. The Swiss constitution is much clearer on the subject of *human dignity*, as Article 7 states: "Human dignity must be respected and protected." (In German, the sentence is "Die Würde des Menschen ist zu achten und zu schützen," which has an even better ring to it.) On the subject of decapitating flowers without a rational reason, for better or worse Americans still retain the liberty to do so, a point established in the seminal case of Spackler v. Bushwood Country Club (Neb. 1980).